Ham

Go Bag

Max Cooper

Ham Radio Go Bag

Reproduction or translation of any part of this work beyond that permitted by section 107 or 108 of the 1976 United States Copyright Act without permission of the copyright owner is unlawful. The author believes, to the best of his knowledge, that the information provide in this book is correct at the time of this writing. Requests for permission or further information should be addressed to the author.

DISCLAIMER AND/OR LEGAL NOTICES:

Care has been taken to confirm the accuracy of the information presented. However, the author and publisher are not responsible for errors or omissions or for any consequences from application of the information in this book and make no warranty, expressed or implied, with respect to the currency, completeness, or accuracy of the contents of the publication.

Table of Contents

Max Cooper

Introduction

Scenario:

It is 6:12AM on a cold December Thursday morning. I just logged onto my work computer and was checking my email. All of a sudden the power went out for the entire building. Not unusual for such an occurrence to happen every once in a while during the winter months. Probably a winter storm that knocked out a transformer I thought to myself. I looked out the window of my 15th floor office and noticed that the city was completely dark. Buildings were dark, street lights were dark, and apparently the power outage was widespread. The only visible lights where those from vehicles which were now in gridlock because the traffic control lights were not working. The building was being evacuated as a safety measure which meant no elevator. Surprisingly, even the emergency lights in the stairwell did not work. It was literally completely dark. No big deal as I carry a flashlight. Others were using the flashlight on their cell phones for light. In all the previous situations of power outages the emergency lights always worked. Now, everything electric was completely dead. Even my security card access would not work and I could no longer access restricted areas. I made it outside safely.

Once outside I attempted to call my wife but my cellphone would not get a dial tone. I attempted to send a text message…nothing. I attempted to contact her through an app...nothing. I tried to access the internet on my phone...nothing. I was starting to think this is not just a storm but something bigger. No one knew what was happening and everyone had more questions than answers. We were disconnected from electricity, cell phone service and information was immediately a scarce commodity. We were in the dark both literally and figuratively. We had questions but no answers. We had lights but no electricity. We had phones but no service. And, I still did not know what was causing this havoc but more importantly I had no idea on whether my family was safe or not! My mental checklist started to evaluate possibilities:

- *Winter storm...unknown*
- *Major accident...unknown*
- *Equipment failure...unknown*
- *Act of terrorism...unknown*
- *Attack on the electrical grid...unknown*
- *Cyberterrorism...unknown*
- *Unconventional warfare...unknown*
- *Conventional war...unknown*

The bottom line is I had no answers and no way to obtain timely, valuable, accurate and relevant information. I was literally...in the dark!

The dark can be a scary and lonely place...especially for the unprepared!

The last few years has seen a virtual explosion of talk regarding preparedness especially with the popularity of prepper reality shows, magazines, blogs, websites, YouTube channels and social media. People are not only thinking about being more prepared but they are pro-actively taking steps to become more prepared. Yet, one area of preparedness that is typically neglected is in the area of communications, specifically two-way communications. Conducting two-way communication during a known or unknown crisis is commonly referred to as emergency communications or EMCOMM for short. Your ability to remain in contact with loved ones during an emergency or crisis is critical if only for peace of mind knowing that your family is safe. In the event of a societal breakdown your ability to effectively communicate may be the difference between life and death. Two-way communications provides you a means of obtaining valuable information especially if other parts of the grid are down such as television and radio stations which typically report the news. In such an incident the ability to obtain relevant, timely, and accurate information can literally be lifesaving as you can avoid potential travel to dangerous locations or avoid groups of people who may be rioting or causing civil disobedience.

One form of communications that has been proven ineffective time and time again is cellular phone service which is not reliable during a natural disaster or man-made crisis. Still, the majority of people rely exclusively on their cell phone for emergency communications not realizing the limitations. This lack of reliability has multiple causes but there are two main reasons that will concern you. First, the natural disaster may destroy part of the network rendering cell phone calls impossible. Second, even when the network is not damaged the amount of people using the system will very quickly overwhelm its capabilities rendering the system ineffective. This happened during the terrorist events of September 11th attacks and the Boston Marathon bombing. There are also situations where law enforcement may shut down the cellular system for security reasons. While this is rare it can still impact your ability to communicate. If your main form of two-way communication during a crisis is a cellular phone then you are not adequately prepared.

> ***Cell phones are generally not a dependable form of communications during an emergency.***

If a cellphone is your sole emergency communications plan you are setting yourself up for failure.

Many people use the internet as a source of information for emergency preparedness and every other topic imaginable. There are forums, blogs, YouTube channels, webinars, Facebook pages and a host of webpages devoted to every aspect of preparedness. Unfortunately, there is a lot of inaccurate and, in some cases, completely wrong information being provided. Some of the information is in violation of the law which can result in penalties being brought against you. Just because something is posted on the internet does not make it factual. There are so many examples of bad information being provided that a book could be devoted to that topic. When it comes to two-way communications an excellent source of information is the Federal Communications Commission[i] website. Another excellent source of information is the U.S. Government Printing Office which hosts the Electronic Code of Federal Regulations[ii] for amateur radio service and personal radio service. This is where you will find all the rules and regulations that apply to two-way communications. I understand that reading pages of rules and regulations is not the most fun task but it is critical to know and understand this information. The reality is that if you do not know the laws, rules, and regulations then you are more apt to engage in activities that violate these standards. This can lead to problems, including legal problems, which are easily avoidable with a little time and effort. It is your responsibility to know the rules when operating a two-way radio. It is not a justifiable excuse to say, "*But, I saw it on the internet.*"

The internet is a great tool but it is a double edged sword especially if you do not know if the information you are getting is accurate. And while the FCC has authority to hold accountable individuals who break the rules the reality is that you will never be bothered by the FCC unless you are an egregious violator. The truth is that the FCC just does not have the resources and manpower to go after everyone that violates the rules. But this does not mean you should violate the rules just because you may get away with doing so. Be a good amateur radio operator and follow all FCC rules.

> ***Don't believe everything you read on the Internet.***
>
> **Abraham Lincoln**

Target Audience

Amateur radio is a very encompassing and diverse hobby with a wide variety of different capabilities. The depth and breadth of ham radio is truly amazing and can take many years to master. Some ham radio operators tend to have a varied skill set while others remain very focused on specific areas. To state that this is a comprehensive field is an understatement. Many amateur radio groups, books, videos, blogs, tutorials, forums and webpages have been dedicated to the different capabilities of ham radio. You may end up getting into ham radio for a specific purpose and then find out that there are many other areas of interest that grab your attention.

A partial list of the modes of communication include:

Voice

- Amplitude modulation (AM)
- Double Sideband Suppressed Carrier (DSB-SC)
- Independent Sideband (ISB)
- Single Sideband (SSB)
- Amplitude Modulation Equivalent (AME)
- Frequency modulation (FM)
- Phase modulation (PM)

Image

- Amateur Television, also known as Fast Scan television (ATV)
- Slow-Scan Television (SSTV)
- Facsimile

Text and Data

- Continuous Wave (CW) – Morse Code
- ALE Automatic Link Establishment
- AMateur Teleprinting Over Radio (AMTOR)
- D-STAR
- Echolink
- Discrete multi-tone modulation modes such as Multi Tone 63 (MT63)
- Multiple Frequency-Shift Keying (MFSK) modes such as FSK441, JT6M, JT65, and

- Olivia MFSK
- Packet radio (AX25) Automatic Packet Reporting System (APRS)

PACTOR

- PSK31 - Phase-Shift Keying 31 baud binary phase shift keying
- QPSK31 - 31 baud quadrature phase shift keying
- PSK63 - 63 baud binary phase shift keying
- QPSK63 - 63 baud quadrature phase shift keying

Spread Spectrum

- Radioteletype (RTTY)

Modes by Activity

- Earth-Moon-Earth (EME)
- Internet Radio Linking Project (IRLP)
- Low Transmitter Power (QRP)
- Satellite (OSCAR- Orbiting Satellite Carrying Amateur Radio)

Yet, this is a very narrowly focused book on a very specific topic – *individual or small group emergency communications.* The idea is that you are working either independently or with a small group of people that you regularly train in relation to emergency communication.

There are two main groups that this book will appeal towards.

1. Those who are preppers and/or survivalists looking to increase their ability to effectively communicate during a crisis. The information provided in this book will be **_one component_** of their overall plan. The radio items discussed may be incorporated into a traditional "go bag," "bug out bag," or to create a separate communications go bag.

2. Those new to amateur radio who are looking to obtain information on creating a stand-alone ham radio go bag. These individuals may not be as concerned with the "hobby" aspect of amateur radio or capabilities outside of emergency communications. These individuals also may not identify themselves as preppers or survivalists.

This book is not for the hardcore amateur radio enthusiast or hobbyist. If you are an amateur radio operator who participates in EMCOMM groups this book will not be geared toward you although there may be some overlap. Those involved in amateur radio emergency communications groups tend to carry significantly more radio gear, antennas, meters, batteries, power supplies, etc. than will be discussed in this book. Often, all the gear carried in these situations is so heavy and bulky that it requires a vehicle to transport.

Privacy and Two-Way Radio Communications

For the sake of operational security (OpSec) it is a good policy to understand that there is absolutely no privacy with any form of two-way communications to include amateur radio, FRS, GMRS, CB, MURS, Cellular phone, etc. Assume this to be true even if you are using encryption technology which is generally beyond the scope of most users and is not authorized for amateur radio operators. Also, some radios such as FRS/GMRS boast that they have "privacy codes" which have very little to do with actual privacy. Even when using FRS/GMRS privacy codes your conversation is not private and can be heard by others. There are some radios that claim to have encrypted, private and secure communications. Keep in mind that these radios are very expensive and even these can be defeated with advanced electronic equipment and software. Such technology is typically available to government agencies. Chances are you are not important enough to have the government actively listening to your conversations but there is always the possibility.

> The bottom line is that you should conduct yourself as if your conversations are being heard by others. Maintain the mindset that nothing you say is secure and all conversations can be heard by a third party. When using amateur radio all of your conversations are an open book so act accordingly.

Additionally, according to FCC Rule, **§97.113 Prohibited Transmissions[iii]:**

(4) ...; **messages encoded for the purpose of obscuring their meaning**, except as otherwise provided herein; obscene or indecent words or language; or false or deceptive messages, signals or identification.

When using your ham radio you cannot encode, disguise, or obscure the message that is being transmitted. The bottom line is that, according to FCC rules, your message is to be clear and not coded.

Two-Way Radio Communication – Amateur Radio

This book is going to be limited to amateur radio and will not cover FRS, GMRS, CB, or MURS. Yet, it is important to briefly discuss their capabilities. The reason only amateur radio is covered is because it is the most effective form of two-way communication compared to the other options. This is not to say that other forms of two-way communications do not have their place among your gear. All of them have their own strengths and weaknesses that will vary depending on your situation and needs. For example, FRS/GMRS radios are not good to communicate over a long distance. Yet, in your particular case you may only need to communicate with a family members over a short distance of say ½ mile. In this case the FRS/GMRS radios may fit your needs perfectly. The key is to understand your needs regarding communicating during a crisis and then using the correct radio equipment.

It is common to find FRS/GMRS radios combined into one radio and then advertised as "Up to 36 Miles" for communications. If you read the small print it states that obtaining 36 miles is under optimal conditions that, for the most part, are unrealistic. I have yet to meet anyone who was able to obtain 15 miles from such a radio. I have conducted numerous tests with different brand radios and 2 miles seems to be the best I am able to obtain. CB radios are good for about 4 miles on average. With a MURS radio you can get 1-5 miles and you can extend that range to about 10 miles connecting the unit to an external antenna. Amateur radio is in a whole other league regarding communication capabilities. With a 5 watt handy talky (HT) I have been able to communicate over 2,200 miles using a linked repeater system. And the quality of the communications was crystal clear. The radio I was using was a basic Yaesu FT-60 which is, in my opinion, one of the best entry level amateur radio's you can get. Depending on your license, equipment, and skill level it is safe to say you can talk to any part of the world with an amateur radio.

Two-Way Radio communication comparison chart:

	Watts	Channels	License Required	Cost of License	Term of License
FRS	.5	14	N	-	-
GMRS	1-5 Mobile 50 Base	23	Y	$85*	5 Years
CB	4 - AM 12 - SSB	40	N	-	-
MURS	2	5	N	-	-
Amateur Radio	1-5 Mobile 1500+ Base	A Lot	Y	$15 to test	10 Years

* In 2010, the FCC proposed to remove the individual licensing requirement for GMRS and instead license GMRS "by rule" (meaning that an individual license would not be required to operate a GMRS device). This proposal is still pending.[iv]

Based on the previous chart it becomes very obvious that amateur radio clearly provides the most capabilities for two-way communications. In fact, none of the other listed options even come close to ham radio capability. This makes it the primary choice for two-way communications especially for emergency situations.

Amateur radio is a very large and diverse field with numerous levels of licenses. The current levels from the lowest to the highest are: Technician, General, and Extra. There are some older classifications still around such as Novice but these will be irrelevant if you are going for your license. Additionally, Morse code is <u>NO longer required</u> for testing. If you want the most capability to communicate over a long distance you really must consider obtaining your Technician's license. It is a 35 question test and all of the test questions and answers are available for free on the Internet. There are also online practice exams that you can take for free.[v] With a little time, motivation, and effort you can easily pass the test thereby dramatically increasing your communication ability.

Regarding the distance you will get with any radio it is important to understand that there are a lot of variables that impact the effectiveness of ALL radios. Such variables include: Number of watts, antenna, weather conditions, location, obstructions, operating knowledge of your equipment, radio quality, etc. All of these are important factors in helping to determine which set up will fit your requirements.

According to the American Radio Relay League (ARRL) in 2012, *"The number of radio amateurs in the US reached an all-time high of almost 710,000."*[vi] While not all of these radio operators are currently active there is still a very large interest in amateur radio. In part, I believe this increase of licensed amateur radio operators must be due to the increase in "prepper" related topics that are currently so prevalent. Time will tell if this trend will remain or if it is going to be a passing fad. Whether this is a passing fad or not there are many individuals who currently are licensed amateur radio operators who want to be prepared for big and small emergencies. It is important to remember that amateur radio is one form of communications that has been proven both reliable and effective in times of emergencies. This is what makes amateur radio such a huge asset and skill to develop.

The focus of this book is creating a **Ham Radio Go Bag** that is:

- Portable with a handheld radio (HT)

- Mobile (Easy to transport and carry)

- Simple

- Small

- Lightweight

- Effective

There are many aspects to amateur radio and it is a very diverse hobby with a lot of different capabilities. There are many ways to define and develop a "go bag" ranging from very small to uniquely large and cumbersome. My focus is on the *individual licensed amateur radio operator* who is not necessarily part of a disaster response team, Community Emergency Response Team (CERT), Amateur Radio Emergency Service® (ARES[vii]), or Radio Amateur Civil Emergency Services (RACES[viii].) Since the focus is on individuals who are not necessarily part of a larger response team the contents of your go bag may be significantly different than if you were volunteering at an event or as part of an emergency disaster team. In order to help define your needs for an amateur radio go bag you need to conduct an assessment to determine the contents of your bag. The "go bag" outlined in this book is geared toward the individual or small group of individuals who want to maintain radio communications for emergency purposes which may be local, regional, national or global. Any ham radio go bag that you develop must meet needs that you anticipate depending on your circumstances. This means that a go bag you develop may be significantly different from a go bag that another amateur radio user develops. Always develop a bag that is uniquely your own and not because someone else carries a certain type of radio or piece of gear. If you do not create your go bag based on your needs and requirements then do not expect it to benefit you when you need it the most.

Communications Assessment

One of the first and most important steps for you is to accurately and realistically determine your needs in relation to emergency two-way communications. Without conducting such an assessment you may find yourself spending money on improper equipment that fails to fit your needs. This will not serve you well in a crisis. Skipping this step will more than likely be expensive in the long run as you may end up purchasing radio equipment that you do not need, or worse, do not fit your requirements.

Answer the following questions to help determine your needs.

1. Do you have a <u>written</u> emergency communications plan?

   a) If yes, do you practice your plan on a regular basis?

   _____ Yes   _____ No

2. Who are you primarily going to communicate with during a crisis?

3. What is the purpose of your communication?

4. What is the longest distance you are going to need to communicate? (Critical Question)

   _____

5. What type of environment do you live?

   Urban   Suburban   Rural   Isolated

   Other: _____

6. What is the terrain like where you live?

   Open   Mountains   Forest   Desert   Water

   Other: _____

7. Are you going to be in one location, mobile, or a combination of both?

8. What kind of power supply do you plan on having for your equipment?

Ham Radio Go Bag

Depending on your situation you may come up with a host of other relevant questions to determine your two-way radio communication needs. Take the time *up front* to really give adequate thought to what your needs are relating to emergency communications and the development of your ham radio go bag. The answers that you come up with will eventually determine how your go bag is designed and implemented. This process can also save you a lot of time and money because you know exactly what your needs are and can purchase radio equipment and gear that will compliment your needs.

> **Having a written emergency communications plan is a critical element to your emergency preparedness. Without a well written plan that is practiced you are essentially "winging it" during a bad situation. Generally, this tactic tends not to be effective and has consequences.**
>
> **Do NOT skip this step.**

FAMILY EMERGENCY COMMUNICATIONS PLAN

Emergency Phone Numbers:

Contact	Phone Number
Police, Fire, Paramedics, Ambulance	9-1-1
Poison Control Center (U.S.)	800-222-1222

Emergency Meeting Location:

Location		Notes
1. Primary Near Home		
2. Secondary		
3. Out of Town		

Family Contacts:

Family Member	Cell Phone	Alternate Phone	E-Mail
1.			
2.			
3.			
4.			
5.			

Secondary Emergency Contacts:

Secondary Contact	Cell Phone	Alternate Phone	E-Mail
1.			
2.			
3.			
4.			
5.			

Out of State Contacts:

Out of State Contact	Cell Phone	Alternate Phone	E-Mail
1.			
2.			
3.			

It is always interesting to hear people say that they have a ham radio for: Emergency communications, SHTF, WROL, TEOTWAWKI, and the apocalypse. But when asked what their emergency communications plan consist of they state they do not have such a plan. It does not make sense to have an emergency form of communications yet not have a written plan.

It is the emergency communications plan that drives so much of your decisions on what type of radio and accessories to purchase. This in turn determines your capabilities and potential effectiveness to communicate. Your ability to effectively and efficiently communicate with others will provide you with valuable intelligence and information that can then assist with decisions and actions.

Without a written emergency communications plan you are essentially improvising during a crisis. This is probably not the best course of action to take when lives may be in jeopardy. Without a written and well-practiced plan you will more than likely fail at your objective if you even know what your objective is. As the saying goes:

Failing to plan is planning to fail.

Do not expect your improvisation to get you through an emergency unscathed. The costs may be high and the consequences lifelong. The ability to improvise is important in a crisis and tends to work best when it is based off a plan that is understood and practiced.

Ham Radio Go Bag

Amateur Radio Service

Amateur radio operators have a long and proud tradition of being essential during emergencies. As a result there are numerous FCC rules for providing emergency communication. Even if you are building a ham radio go bag for your individualized needs or that of a small group it is still beneficial to be aware of the rules that are in place. Some of the more relevant FCC rules relating to emergency communications are listed below.

According to the FCC Public Safety and Homeland Security Bureau[ix]:

> *"The FCC established amateur radio as a voluntary, non-commercial, radio communications service. It allows licensed operators to improve their communications and technical skills, while providing the nation with a pool of trained radio operators and technicians who can provide essential communications during emergencies."*

Subpart E—Providing Emergency Communications

§97.403 Safety of life and protection of property[x]

No provision of these rules prevents the use by an amateur station of any means of radio communication at its disposal to provide essential communication needs in connection with the immediate safety of human life and immediate protection of property when normal communication systems are not available.

§97.405 Station in distress

(a) No provision of these rules prevents the use by an amateur station in distress of any means at its disposal to attract attention, make known its condition and location, and obtain assistance.

(b) No provision of these rules prevents the use by a station, in the exceptional circumstances described in paragraph (a) of this section, of any means of radio communications at its disposal to assist a station in distress.

§97.407 Radio amateur civil emergency service

(a) No station may transmit in RACES unless it is an FCC-licensed primary, club, or military recreation station and it is certified by a civil defense organization as registered with that organization. No person may be the control operator of an amateur station transmitting in RACES unless that person holds a FCC-issued amateur operator license and is certified by a civil defense organization as enrolled in that organization.

(b) The frequency bands and segments and emissions authorized to the control operator are available to stations transmitting communications in RACES on a shared basis with the amateur service. In the event of an emergency which necessitates invoking the President's War Emergency Powers under the provisions of section 706 of the Communications Act of 1934, as amended, 47 U.S.C. 606, amateur stations participating in RACES may only transmit on the frequency segments authorized pursuant to part 214 of this chapter.

(c) An amateur station registered with a civil defense organization may only communicate with the following stations upon authorization of the responsible civil defense official for the organization with which the amateur station is registered:

(1) An amateur station registered with the same or another civil defense organization; and

(2) A station in a service regulated by the FCC whenever such communication is authorized by the FCC.

(d) All communications transmitted in RACES must be specifically authorized by the civil defense organization for the area served. Only civil defense communications of the following types may be transmitted:

(1) Messages concerning impending or actual conditions jeopardizing the public safety, or affecting the national defense or security during periods of local, regional, or national civil emergencies;

(2) Messages directly concerning the immediate safety of life of individuals, the immediate protection of property, maintenance of law and order, alleviation of human suffering and need, and the combating of armed attack or sabotage;

(3) Messages directly concerning the accumulation and dissemination of public information or instructions to the civilian population essential to the activities of the civil defense organization or other authorized governmental or relief agencies; and

(4) Communications for RACES training drills and tests necessary to ensure the establishment and maintenance of orderly and efficient operation of the RACES as ordered by the responsible civil defense organization served. Such drills and tests may not exceed a total time of 1 hour per week. With the approval of the chief officer for emergency planning in the applicable State, Commonwealth, District or territory, however, such tests and drills may be conducted for a period not to exceed 72 hours no more than twice in any calendar year.

As you can see there are very specific rules for RACES and use of amateur radio for emergency transmissions. While the focus of this book is geared towards individuals or small groups of individuals it is still important to at least be exposed to some of these regulations. You may also get the interest in serving your community in times of disaster where your radio skills will be a significant asset.

Getting your Amateur Radio License

If you are not currently an amateur radio operator you are probably wondering what the process is to become licensed. The rules are listed below. Fortunately, obtaining your ham radio license is actually pretty easy if you put in some time and studying. If you are currently licensed you can skip this short section.

Subpart F—Qualifying Examination Systems[xi]

§97.501 Qualifying for an amateur operator license

Each applicant must pass an examination for a new amateur operator license grant and for each change in operator class. Each applicant for the class of operator license grant specified below must pass, or otherwise receive examination credit for, the following examination elements:

(a) Amateur Extra Class operator: Elements 2, 3, & 4;

(b) General Class operator: Elements 2 and 3;

(c) Technician Class operator: Element 2.

Ham Radio Go Bag

§97.503 Element standards

A written examination must be such as to prove that the examinee possesses the operational and technical qualifications required to perform properly the duties of an amateur service licensee. Each written examination must be comprised of a question set as follows:

(a) Element 2: 35 questions concerning the privileges of a Technician Class operator license. The minimum passing score is 26 questions answered correctly.

(b) Element 3: 35 questions concerning the privileges of a General Class operator license. The minimum passing score is 26 questions answered correctly.

(c) Element 4: 50 questions concerning the privileges of an Amateur Extra Class operator license. The minimum passing score is 37 questions answered correctly.

For more information on licensing, education and training related to amateur radio visit the ARRL website at:

http://www.arrl.org/licensing-education-training

Once you obtain your ham radio license, also referred to as your "ticket," you can choose what type of radio or radios you want to purchase. There are three main types of radios to choose from which include:

- Base station – Typically a larger and more powerful unit that remains in your home.

Some base stations provide up to 1,500 watts.

- Mobile – Radio that is generally installed in your vehicle. Some individuals carry mobile radios in a go bag but this requires a power source that is typically larger and a bit more cumbersome. Mobile stations typically provide 50-100 watts.

- Handheld Portable – Also known as "Handy Talkies (HT)" radios these are very small and portable radios that are easy to carry with you. This type of radio will be the primary focus of the type of radio to carry in your go bag. HT radios are typically a maximum of 5 watts.

Each type of radio whether base station, mobile or handy talkie have both pros and cons. Again, this is why it is important to complete the communications assessment to determine your specific needs. Many ham radio operators have all three types of radios to provide complete coverage whether they are at home, on the road, or camping, hiking or backpacking.

New amateur radio operators begin with the Technician Class license. According to the ARRL[xii]:

"The FCC Technician License exam covers basic regulations, operating practices and electronics theory, with a focus on VHF and UHF applications. Morse code is not required for this license. With a Technician Class license, you will have all ham radio privileges above 30 MHz. These privileges include the very popular 2-meter band. Many Technician licensees enjoy using small (2 meter) hand-held radios to stay in touch with other hams in their area. Technicians may operate FM voice, digital packet (computers), television, single-sideband voice and several other interesting modes. You can even make international radio contacts via satellites, using relatively simple station equipment. Technician licensees now also have additional privileges on certain HF frequencies. Technicians may also operate on the 80, 40 and 15 meter bands using CW, and on the 10 meter band using CW, voice and digital modes."

Many new ham radio operators with a Technicians level license will spend a lot of time operating on the 2M and 70cm bands.

These cover the following frequencies:

- **2M (144MHz): 144.0 – 148.0   VHF**

- **70cm (420MHz): 420.0 – 450.0   UHF**

Almost all handy talkie radios will have either one or both of these frequency bands on the radio. And while these frequencies are typically not known for very long distance communications you can use a "linked repeater system" which will allow you to communicate over thousands of miles with repeaters that are linked together. This will dramatically increase your communication range. A repeater is a relay device that is a specially designed transceiver which instantly retransmits signals heard in their receivers. To be most effective repeaters are generally located on the roofs of tall buildings or at the summits of hills or mountains. The majority repeaters operate on the 2 meter and 70 cm bands.

As with most things in life there are pros and cons. Amateur radio is no exception and listed below are some common pros and cons to this communications medium.

Amateur Radio Pros:

- + Long distance communications

- + Ham radio operators tend to be more technically proficient with their equipment

- + Can utilize a repeater and linked repeaters to dramatically increase your communications range

Ham Radio Go Bag

+ Ability to operate using simplex or repeaters

+ Various data types (voice, text, data, photos, documents, e-mail, television)

+ Can use different antennas to increase performance

+ A lot of radio options are available

+ Base stations can transmit 1,500 watts (Not the focus of this book)

+ Some radio models have a lot of different functionality and user options such as GPS

+ Can use Morse code (not required for licensing purposes)

+ Can connect to global positioning system (GPS) and automated position reporting system (APRS)

+ License is for a 10 year period

Amateur Radio Cons:

− Requires a license (Can be viewed as a pro)

- More technical than FRS/GMRS, CB radio, etc. so there is a learning curve

- Quality equipment can be more expensive

- Communications are not private

- Handhelds are limited to 5 watts

- Your station can be inspected by the FCC (Very rare probability)

- Cannot transmit coded messages or messages with hidden meanings which can be problematic depending on the situation and type of emergency

- Must identify your station at least every 10 minutes which means that others can learn your true identity

The pros of ham radio far outweigh the cons. Having a reliable form of communications oftentimes with crystal clear clarity over a long distance can literally be a lifesaver during an emergency.

Ham Radio Go Bag

Radio Go Bag

Now that you are familiar with some of the FCC rules relating to emergency communications and you have completed your "Communications Assessment" it is now time to move to the action phase and do the following:

- Write a written emergency communications plan (Do not skip this vital step)

- Research and purchase appropriate equipment based on your specific and individualized needs

- Choose a bag platform to carry your radio gear.

- Put together your ham radio go bag

- Train with the plan that you have developed and the equipment that you have purchased. It is only through realistic training that you will discover the holes in your plan which will then require modification to fix any deficiencies.

The training component is very important. Too many people build a go bag and fail to train with the components. They assume that when something goes wrong that they will pull out their gear and everything will operate smoothly. This is rarely the case and stresses the importance of conducting regular training to determine the strengths and weaknesses of your setup. Additionally, once your bag is set up it should be what I refer to as a "dynamic" set up meaning that you will continually modify and reevaluate your set up as needed. You should never build a go bag and then just assume that it is always good to go. New products hit the market and technology changes meaning that you will need to change as required in order to have the most effective go bag possible.

At this point I want to reiterate my thought process on developing a ham radio go bag so that we are on the same page. This is especially important because there are many different types of radio go bag set ups that you can choose depending on your needs. For example, if you work ARES or RACES your set up may be very different from the one I will discuss. The go bag set up discussed in this book is:

- Based on a 5 watt handy talkie (HT)

- Mobile

- Simple

- Relatively small

- Lightweight

- Effective

For some of you these parameters may not fit your needs. This is not a problem as all you need to do is apply the thought process to your individualized needs in order to develop a go bag that will work for your situation. Many individuals, especially new hams, will use a 2M / 70cm radio. But, if you have an Extra license you may want to use a quad band handy talkie that provides more communications options with increased band and frequency availability.

It is also important to point out that I am ONLY focusing on the radio aspect of a go bag and not necessarily everything that you would include in a normal go bag. This is not to imply that you should not have all of the other items in order to have a complete system. If needed, you can refer to my prior books called, "Realistic Bug Out Bag," "Realistic Everyday Carry," or "Everyday Carry: 5.11 Tactical PUSH Pack" for more information.

Equipment Recommendations

Before you spend a dime on radio equipment it is imperative that you have a written plan that determines the equipment that you will purchase. Do not buy radio equipment first and then develop a plan because your plan may call for different equipment. Once you know what equipment you want I recommend obtaining only high quality radios. I realize that times are tough and it may require time to obtain what you need. But, the reality is that you may skimp on quality equipment and find yourself in the middle of a crisis with equipment that does not work. Quality comes with a price tag but I find that the expense is well worth the cost in terms of performance, durability, quality, and effectiveness. I have purchased and used inexpensive radios and NONE of them perform as well as a name brand quality radio. When it comes to purchasing a radio I recommend buying a name brand such as Yaesu, Kenwood or Icom. This is not to say that there are no other brands available but these three companies have a proven record of quality which is exactly what you want and need in a crisis.

It is also important to warn you against carrying too much gear. Ham radio operators love their radios and complimentary gear. The problem is that the size and weight of your pack will rapidly get out of control. You must also realize that your radio go bag may only be one component of your overall set up. For example, if you carry an everyday carry (EDC) set up then you are already carrying other gear in addition to your radio. If you plan on bugging out you will have much more gear than just your radio. Size and weight are always factors to consider. Now, if you are just going to be carrying a radio go bag and a few extra items you might have a little more leeway in terms of what you can include in your bag. More does not always equate to better so really decide if the items you carry are a want or a need. Also remember that if you actually train with your go bag you will find out what works and what does not work. This will allow you to modify your radio go bag to meet your needs.

Handy Talkie (HT) Radios

When it comes to choosing a HT radio there are a lot of options but I am sticking with the top three name brands mainly because I need a radio that I can count on when needed. There are other radios available for you to research but I do recommend steering clear of the inexpensive Chinese radios that have quality control issues and often fail to put out the number of advertised watts. If involved in the worst case scenario you are going to want radio equipment that is reliable, dependable, and durable. You may need to count on this radio in an emergency situation when your life or the life of a loved one is in danger.

When it comes to choosing a radio I do not recommend going with a single band radio because it is too limiting. At a minimum I recommend a dual band 2M and 70cm radio which provides more options. If you have a General or Extra class license you should consider a triband or quad band radio so that you have access to different bands. Again, you have to determine which radio will best meet your needs which may also be dependent on the level of your amateur radio license. Recommended HT radios:

Yaesu:

Model	Band	Ave. Price
FT-60	2M / 70cm	$149.99
VX-6R	2M / 220 MHz / 70cm	$239.95
VX-8DR	2M / 220 MHz / 70cm / 6M	$339.95
VX-8GR	2M / 70cm	$379.95
FT1DR	2M / 70cm	$309.95
FT2DR	2M / 70cm	$549.95

Kenwood:

Model	Band	Ave. Price
TH-F6A	2M / 220 MHz / 70cm	$319.95
TH-D72A	2M / 70cm	$449.95

Icom:

Model	Band	Ave. Price
IC-T70A HD	2M / 70cm	$209.95
ID-51A PLUS	2M / 70cm	$399.95

- **Yaesu FT-60 Dual Band Handheld 5W VHF / UHF Amateur Radio Transceiver**

I routinely use the Yaesu FT-60 radio and feel that this radio performs well for my needs. It is the lowest price HT radio of the ones I listed and typically costs about $149.00. It is a basic, well-built, durable, and dependable dual band radio. It lacks a lot of the bells and whistles of more modern radios. I use a simple amateur radio and do not need GPS, APRS, beaconing, sending packets, sending photos, etc. This basic radio is all I need for most situations so it is the radio that I have dedicated to my ham radio go bag. If you need other capabilities there are definitely other radio options to consider.

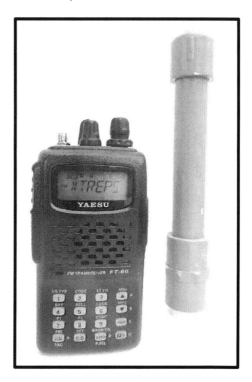

The Yaesu FT-60 DualBand Handheld 5W VHF/UHF Amateur Radio Transceiver - Dual Band is an excellent radio especially for new ham radio operators. Whether you are looking for a handy talkie (HT) for a hobby, emergency communications (EMCOMM), or for those times when cell phone service is not reliable the Yaesu FT-60 is an excellent choice. At 5 watts it is also a good option when hiking, backpacking, or camping. Preppers will find this to be a useful form of communications. This is also a great radio for a ham radio go bag. Generally, I do NOT carry this radio with me. I only carry my ham radio go bag when there is an indication that I may need the radio based upon local weather conditions, local events, national or international events, or other situations where I feel the radio is worth carrying. If I am traveling a long distance by vehicle I always carry my radio go bag with me even though I have a mobile ham radio in my vehicle. The reason for this is because I may need to leave the vehicle and travel on foot. In such cases I want a ham radio with me. I have all of the 2M and 70cm repeaters in my state programmed into the radio.

Pros:

+ 5 Watts of Power
+ 1000 Memory Channels
+ Dual band VHF/UHF for 2M and 70cm bands
+ NOAA Weather Alerts
+ User manual is well written
+ High quality; durable product
+ Decent battery life (the battery is good for approximately 300 charges)

41

+ Sound clarity is very good
+ Lots of accessories are available
+ The radio has a lot of options and functions to change different settings to your preference
+ Easy to program although I do recommend using Yaesu ADMS-1J Programming Software which is simple, fast, and effective to program all of your frequencies
+ With a cloning cable it is easy to clone another FT-60 to transfer all of your frequencies

Cons:

- A bit heavy and bulky compared to newer radios
- The speaker volume is a tad bit low for me. Don't get me wrong it is not bad but I would prefer the speaker volume to be a little louder.
- The wall wart charger does not indicate that the radio is charging or when the charge is complete. I upgraded to the Yaesu Vertex-Standard Desktop Rapid Charger which does indicate charge status. Many of the new FT-60's now include this charger when purchasing this radio.
- If you are not using WIRES then turn it off otherwise you will have a delay when pressing the PTT which can cut off what you are saying. Press the "0" (zero) button to disable WIRES.

Recommendations:

1. I recommend upgrading the antenna. Generally, I use the Diamond SRH77CA and notice a significant increase in performance compared to the standard rubber duck antenna. I store the antenna in a PVC case that I constructed.

2. I also recommend getting the Vertex Standard Alkaline Battery Case (FBA-25) which will allow you to use 6 AA alkaline batteries for power should your NiMH battery lose its power. Yaesu does not recommend using Lithium or rechargeable AA batteries with this radio. I do know ham radio operators who use Eneloop rechargeable batteries and have not encountered any problems. If you do choose to use rechargeable batteries you do so at your own risk.

While this radio doesn't have all of the latest and greatest gadgetry such as GPS the FT-60 is a very popular radio that has been around for quite some time and has a proven track record. Many experienced ham operators own one and this is a great first radio. Also, many Community Emergency Response Teams (CERT) use this radio. The FT-60 is often used as a great basic emergency communications (EMCOMM) radio. Keep in mind that during a crisis such as 9/11 and the Boston Marathon bombing cell phone service failed yet ham radio operators where still able to communicate with ease!

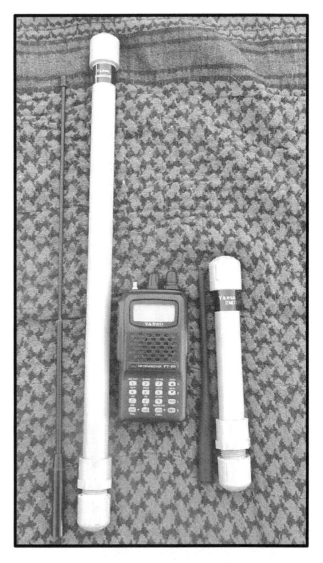

Radio performance has a lot of different variables that will affect how well the radio performs. Your location, type of antenna, battery level, radio settings, etc. can influence radio performance. I am in an area with a lot of repeaters. Using repeaters I have communicated with "nets" from Arizona to California covering hundreds of miles. I am also able to communicate with a friend, using a repeater, which is about 35 miles away. Additionally, I have used a "linked" repeater system that allowed me to communicate from Arizona to Rhode Island covering a distance over 2,500 miles. The sound quality was as good as face-to-face communication. That is pretty amazing considering I was using a 5 watt Yaesu FT-60 HT radio on the 2M band.

Yaesu is a well-known brand in the amateur radio world. They make solid reliable radios that will perform well and last for years. I did a lot of research before purchasing this radio and I have no regrets at all. I would buy this radio again. If you are new to ham radio and don't want to spend a lot of money to get into this hobby the FT-60 is a great radio at a solid price. If you feel you need more functionality than the FT-60 offers you have many other radio options to choose from but stick with a name brand.

Antenna

A quality antenna can make or break your ability to communicate. I highly recommending having a minimum of two antenna's for whatever radio you choose to carry.

It is also important to take care of the antennas as the radio will not work without this vital piece of gear. I like to protect my antennas with a homemade case made out of PVC pipe and accessories which typically costs about $2.50 to make and takes less than 10 minutes to construct.

I carry three antennas in my kit consisting of the following:

Ham Radio Go Bag

- Stock antenna

    I find that the stock antenna performs fairly well
    and I have no complaints. Again, I am located in an
    area with a lot of repeaters so it is not too difficult to hit
    a repeater. If you live in an area that does not have
    many repeaters you would be wise to upgrade your
    antenna.

- Diamond SRH77CA

    The Diamond SRH77CA 144/440 MHz Dual-
    Band High Gain Handheld Antenna is a great upgrade
    from the stock antenna. I compared this antenna with
    the stock antenna and did notice a significant
    improvement with both transmission and reception. I
    was able to hit some repeaters that I was not able to hit
    with the stock antenna and was able to receive better
    reception. This would be expected as this antenna has
    a 15 inch length. Being that the antenna is much longer
    than the stock antenna it can be a bit more challenging
    to store the antenna depending on what type of
    platform that you use for your go bag. It is a bit more
    cumbersome if you are using your radio in the field. I
    do not find this to be a huge issue but it should be
    noted. This antenna is pretty flexible and will not get
    caught up if it hits a fence, branch or other item. I use
    this antenna quite often and I am very pleased with the
    results.

- Maldol Stubby "Soft" 3" Dual Band Amateur Radio Antenna, Model number: MH-209SMA

   The Stubby "Soft" 3" Dual Band Amateur Radio Transceiver & Hand Held Scanner 'SMA' Antenna by Maldol is a fairly decent 2M and 70cm antenna that I use in conjunction with my Yaesu FT-60. Because this is a very small antenna do not have unreasonable expectations regarding performance. Having said that I have been very impressed with this antenna and have been able to hit all of the repeaters that I normally hit with the stock antenna. I hit a repeater that is 32 miles away from inside my house. Pretty impressive for such a small antenna. The antenna is smaller than I anticipated and very pliable.

   One area that I think this antenna can excel if for simplex communications when hiking, backpacking or camping and you are with other radio operators where distance is not going to be an issue. In such situations you do not need to hit a distant repeater. Because this is a very small antenna it is also great to have as a backup antenna if something were to happen to your primary antenna. This antenna is so small and takes very little space in your go bag. There is no reason not to carry this antenna even if it is just as a last resort back up.

Antennas:

Left: Maldol Stubby "Soft" 3" Dual Band
Middle: Stock Antenna
Right: Diamond SRH77CA High Gain Antenna

Radio Accessories

Following is a list of accessories for your radio that you may consider implementing into your ham radio go bag. Feel free to add items that I do not have listed as long as they fit your needs. Keep in mind that each item you carry has a size, weight, and utility component. Choose your gear wisely.

- **Copy of your FCC Amateur Radio License**

  Once you obtain your amateur radio license you can go to the FCC Universal Licensing System[xiii] website and print out an official copy of your amateur radio license. When you print out this license it will have a large license and a wallet size card. I highly recommend laminating the wallet size card and keeping a copy with you at all time and placing one in your radio go bag as well.

- **Copy of your Emergency Communications Plan (ECP)**

  Having a copy of your ECP is important so that you have all the information you need in one place. Oftentimes your ECP will have a lot of information that you would not be able to remember so keep it in your go bag.

- **Radio User Manual**

  Carrying your radios user manual will depend on your skill level with the radio that you carry. If you are very familiar with all of the radios functions you do not need to carry the user manual. But, if you have not used your radio a lot or you are not familiar with all of the radios operations it is a good idea to keep the manual with you. A better option is to thoroughly understand your radio. In reality, you are probably not going to refer to the user manual in a crisis situation. Creating a cheat sheet to guide you through some of the more complicated functions might be a better option than carrying the user manual. Keep in mind there is no substitute for training and practicing with your chosen radio.

- **Extra Batteries**

Since the focus of the radio go bag is one that is light and mobile you are not going to carry a larger radio that requires more power. Yet, even with a HT radio you will need extra batteries to keep you up in running especially if the event lasts longer than you anticipated. I recommend carrying at least two extra batteries for your radio. In addition, it is also a good idea to carry a battery case. I carry the Vertex Standard Alkaline Battery Case (FBA-25). The case is small, lightweight, very easy to carry and holds six AA batteries. Keep in mind that AA batteries will not provide the same output or last as long as the original NiMH battery. I recommend carrying a minimum of 12 AA batteries which will provide you with an emergency power supply if your other radio batteries lose power. Yaesu claims that you should only use alkaline batteries although I know people that use rechargeable batteries. While batteries are small and easy to carry you also need to protect them from getting damaged by wrapping them well or putting them in some type of protective case such as a battery caddy.

- **Cords**

  There are a variety of cords that you may choose to carry. I carry a Yaesu CT-27 Cloning Cable just in case I need to transfer frequencies from another radio operator or they need to copy my frequencies. The cable is very small, lightweight and portable so it is worth having in the go bag.

  I also carry a Yaesu Handheld to PL259 Cable-SMA male plug to UHF female Coaxial Jumper connects to UHF Mobile and Base Antennas. While I do not carry a mobile or base antenna this cable is small and light enough to carry just in case I link up with another radio operator who does carry such an antenna.

- **Cigarette Lighter Plug**

  I include the Yaesu Standard 12V DC Adapter For Handheld Transceivers SDD-13 E-DC-5B in my bag as another power source. Chances are there will typically be a vehicle nearby, depending on your location, which you can use to power your radio.

Yaesu Standard 12V DC Adapter

This DC Adapter is light and does not take up a lot of space. Yet, depending on the emergency situation that you encounter this may be a very handy item to keep your radio powered. Having a power source is one of those things you can never take for granted. This is an item that it is better to have and not need than to need it and not have it. Otherwise, you may end up with a radio paper weight.

- **List of Frequencies**

It is good practice to include a list of frequencies that you have programmed into your radio. As with your license I recommend that your frequency list is laminated or at least protected from the elements such as rain.

Example:

Ch #	RX Freq	TX Freq	Offset Freq	Offset Direction	Name	Tone Mode	CTCSS
1	Open	Open					
2	145.310	144.710	600 kHz	Minus	AJO-MT	Tone	100.0 Hz
3	442.525	447.525	5.00 MHz	Plus	ANTHEM	Tone	114.8 Hz
4	146.820	146.220	600 kHz	Minus	BANK-1	Tone	162.2 Hz
5	447.750	442.750	5.00 MHz	Minus	BELLBT	Tone	100.0 Hz
6	146.780	146.180	600 kHz	Minus	BILLW1	Tone	91.5 Hz
7	449.750	444.750	5.00 MHz	Minus	BILLW2	Tone	91.5 Hz
8	449.975	444.975	5.00 MHz	Minus	BLHDC4	Tone	123.0 Hz
9	146.900	146.300	600 kHz	Minus	BLKCYN	Tone	118.8 Hz
10	146.850	146.250	600 kHz	Minus	BLKPK	Tone	162.2 Hz
11	448.825	443.825	5.00 MHz	Minus	BNSN-1	Tone	107.2 Hz
12	445.300	440.300	5.00 MHz	Minus	BNSN-2	Tone	131.8 Hz
13	147.360	147.960	600 kHz	Plus	BULLH1	Tone	123.0 Hz
14	146.640	146.040	600 kHz	Minus	BULLH2	Tone	123.0 Hz
15	145.170	144.570	600 kHz	Minus	BULLH3	Tone	131.8 Hz

- **Earpiece**

You may choose to utilize an earpiece especially if noise discipline is going to be a factor and you do not want others to be able to hear both sides of your communications. For the Yaesu there is the MH-37A4B Earpiece Microphone, Light Duty. This earpiece fits in one ear and is pretty comfortable and effective.

- **Speaker Microphone**

I'm not a big fan of using the earpiece so instead I use the Yaesu Vertex MH-34B4B Speaker Microphone. The microphone is very small which I like because it does not take up much room. Besides emergency situations this is a good mic to use when hiking, backpacking, or anytime that I need my hands free. The small microphone does not take up much room and you barely notice that it is attached. But, depending on your needs this microphone might not fit the bill. This microphone is a mixed bag as it definitely has some good points and some bad points which will vary depending on your individualized needs.

Pros:

The benefits of this microphone include that it is small, lightweight, and the output quality is very good.

Con:

The plug can come loose from the HT socket. It needs a better way to secure the plug so that it does not come loose especially if you are moving around a lot. It does come with a ring for the antenna but the FT-60 antenna is on the opposite side of the plug so it does not work well in its current design.

- **Cellular Phone and EchoLink**

The reality is that you are probably going to have your cell phone on you whether it is working or not. For most people carrying their cellphone is an engrained habit. EchoLink is a free software that you can download on your computer or an app[xiv] that you can download to your phone. EchoLink provides you the ability to communicate through your computer or cellphone without having a ham radio. According to the EchoLink website regarding their software:

> *"EchoLink® software allows licensed Amateur Radio stations to communicate with one another over the Internet, using streaming-audio technology. The program allows worldwide connections to be made between stations, or from computer to station, greatly enhancing Amateur Radio's communications capabilities. There are more than 200,000 validated users worldwide — in 151 of the world's 193 nations — with about 5,200 online at any given time."*

As you are probably not going to be carrying a laptop with you I will only discuss the app. The EchoLink App by Synergenics, LLC is pretty good although there is a little learning curve and the occasional problem. When you open the app you have the following options to choose:

- ECHOTEST
- Locations
- Repeaters
- Links
- Conferences
- Users
- Recent QSOs

There is a search box at the top of the app for searching: callsign, location or node. At the bottom of the apps are options for:

- QSO
- Text
- Stations
- Favorites
- Settings

I have been able to make numerous contacts and the audio quality was very good. This app will allow you to make contacts worldwide making it a great resource for emergency situations. This app definitely has some utility that you may not be able to get out of a hand held or base station because the app is connect to the internet.

Overall, the EchoLink by Synergenics, LLC app provides a method of using amateur radio operations without having a ham radio. You do need an amateur radio license from the FCC to use the app and your license will be verified. The app provides another option for communication.

Radio Go Bag Platform

After you have determined which radio and radio accessories will fit your emergency needs you will then be ready to obtain a platform to put all of your gear. There are a multitude of options to consider and this is a very individualized choice. Keep in mind that my goal is to be light, fast, and mobile especially considering that my radio go bag may be one component of an overall system. Therefore, I am not looking to carry a lot of radio equipment while still maintaining the ability to conduct effective two-way communications.

Whatever platform you choose to use for your radio gear will have pros and cons. Your goal is to increase the pros and limit the cons. If you are looking for the perfect pack you will be on a never ending quest that will ultimately disappoint you and leave you frustrated. While there may not be a perfect platform make no mistake that there are still a lot of great options available. Take the time to conduct some research before you spend your money and end up with buyer's remorse.

The requirements for my Ham Radio Go Bag are as follows:

- Must be a high quality product that is durable and will last
- Effectively hold the radio, gear and accessories that I carry
- Be relatively comfortable to carry
- Have functional organization

- Can be integrated with a larger pack if
  necessary

When researching which bag or platform is best you want to definitely consider the quality of the item. Look for a bag that uses top quality material, has exceptional stitching and uses quality zippers such as YKK. Another important aspect to consider is the organization of the bag. Make sure that it is large enough to effectively and efficiently hold your gear and that there are enough pockets. Reviewing YouTube product reviews can be a helpful tool to guide you toward a bag that will work for your needs.

Flair

One of the platforms I discuss is the Hazard 4 Tonto Concealed-Carry Mini-Messenger Bag which provides hook and loop area for a patch. This allows you to customize the pack and put some of your personality into your radio go bag. Some may like to put a flag or a patch with your call sign. Keep in mind that whatever "flair" you add to personalize your pack reveals information about you. This is especially true if you have a patch with your call sign as anyone can access the *FCC License Search* website[xv] and look up your call sign. This will provide your name, address and license level. Think before you advertise this information especially if you use your home address on your license instead of a P.O. Box.

Carry-Ability

When choosing a radio go bag you must consider your ability to carry the pack and how comfortable it will be over an extended time period. Personally, I am generally not a big fan of single shoulder packs as they tend to cause shoulder fatigue over time unless the bag is exceptionally light. If your bag is very light this probably will not be an issue but most people tend to overfill their bags which just ends up weighing a lot.

Depending on how you plan on integrating your radio go bag into a larger system such as a bug out bag you may want to consider how this will work. For example:

- Will you place your radio go bag inside your bug out bag?

- Will you attach it using MOLLE webbing?

- Will you use another method to integrate your radio go bag?

Answering these questions may help you decide on what platform to consider and how it will be carried.

DISCLAIMER:

I would like to clearly and unequivocally state that as of this writing I have absolutely no business or personal relationship with Hazard 4 or Maxpedition or any of its employees. I purchased their products and my opinions are solely my own. The information that I provide in this book is completely unbiased and for informational purposes only.

Hazard 4 Tonto[xvi]

According to the Hazard 4 website the follow information is listed regarding the Tonto:

External Size: ~9.4" L x 7.1" W x 4.3" D
(24 x 18 x 11 cm)

Main Compartment: ~9.4" L x 7.1" W x 2.8" D
(24 x 18 x 7 cm)

Main Material: Invista® 1000D Cordura®; PU x2 water repellent coated for superior water resistance.

Colors: Black/Coyote

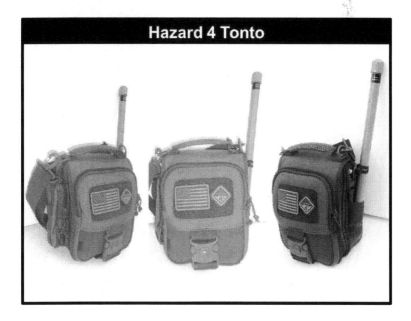

Hazard 4 Tonto

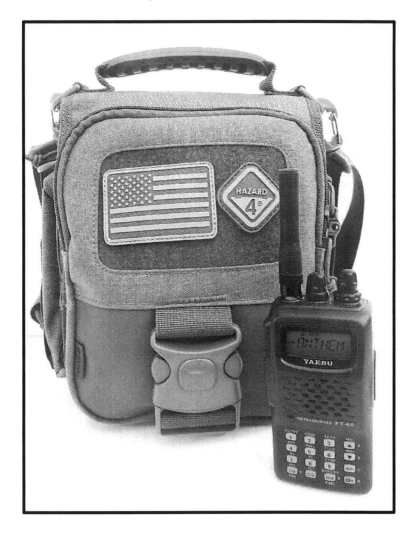

The Hazard 4 Tonto is a well-made mini-messenger bag that works great as a ham radio go bag. It meets all my requirements and I really like this platform because it is simple, lightweight, functional and has good organization. I do not overload this pack so there is room to add more items when needed. All stitching is secure, they YKK zippers work great, buckles are fine, and the shoulder strap is comfortable and well padded. The shoulder strap is adjustable to get a perfect fit for your size. The pack has some MOLLE attachment points to attach additional items but remember this will also add to the bulk of the pack.

All materials and workmanship is not only what you would expect but what you demand from a ham radio go bag platform. This is a pack that should last for many years even with daily use or abuse although I tend to take care of my gear. I have confidence that this pack will survive almost any situation that I can put it through.

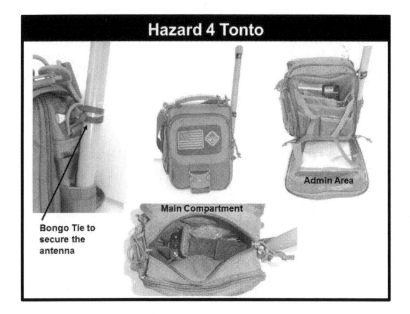

Hazard 4 Tonto

Admin Area

Main Compartment

Bongo Tie to secure the antenna

Carry Handle

The carry handle consists of a flexible rubber like material that has holes on the top side and a unique design on the underside. In the center of the carry handle is a strong nylon strap. The carry handle is described as vented for secure grip even when wet. It is a very nice handle that is easy to grip and very comfortable to carry although most people will probably not use the carry handle as the main transportation mode and will instead use the shoulder strap. But there will always be times when you need to use the carry handle when manipulating the bag, moving it, or when accessing certain pockets. This is a very functional handle that is well made and well designed.

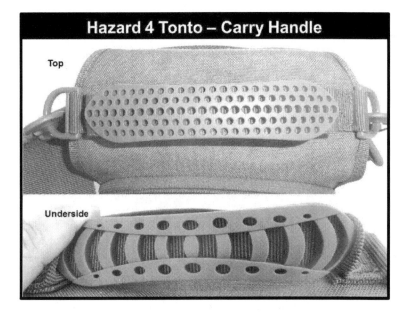

Shoulder Strap with Stabilizer Strap

The Tonto comes with a padded 2 inch shoulder strap that is very comfortable to wear and very easy to adjust so that you get the perfect fit. It also has a removable stabilizer strap for added stability. I normally do not use the stabilizer strap and I removed it. The shoulder straps have swivel hooks made from a durable plastic that has a metal spring loaded latch that is under tension. I would not anticipate a situation where the hook would accidently detach from the D-ring. The shoulder strap can be attached to two sets of D-rings for flap over/under use adding versatility to the manner in which you wear and use the pack. When the pack is closed (front flap down) you would normally use the higher or upper set of D-rings. If you open the front flap and flip it over the bag you would normally use the lower set of D-rings.

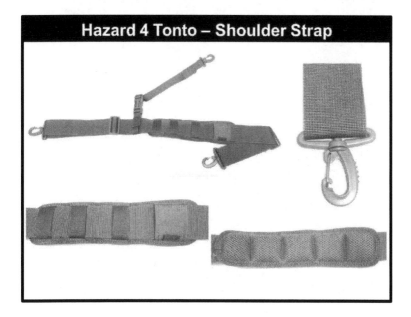

Hazard 4 Tonto – Shoulder Strap

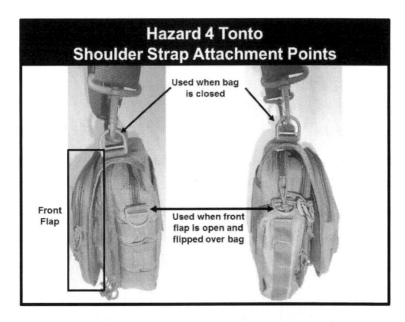

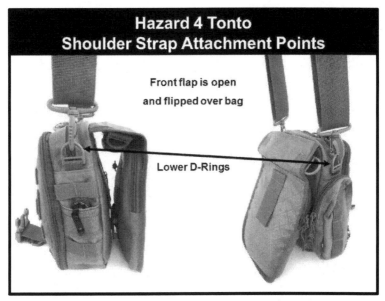

All of the D-rings are made out of plastic yet should be durable enough to last for the life of the bag. I have yet to break any plastic D-ring on any piece of quality gear that I own. If you use lower quality gear the D-rings tend to be less quality and more prone to breaking. This is one of those reasons it is important to buy quality gear. Items may look the same but the build quality is not the same.

There are four MOLLE attachment points on the shoulder pad to either attach items or loop items through the MOLLE. The shoulder strap pad is removable if necessary. Having used a wide variety of gear over the years I find the padded shoulder strap on the Hazard 4 Tonto to be one of the most comfortable due to the thickness of the pad.

Belt Loop

The back side of the Tonto has a belt loop if you choose to attach the pack to your belt for added stability. I do not use the belt look as I feel it limits my mobility and access to the pack. The bottom of the belt loop has Velcro so you do not need to remove your belt to attach the Tonto. You can simply undo the Velcro, put your belt in the slot and then secure the Velcro closed. This is a very simple and fast process. The Velcro strip is relatively small but is secure enough to keep the Tonto in place should you use this carry method. When utilizing this carry method you will still need to use the shoulder strap as the weight of the Tonto with your gear will be too much and too uncomfortable to wear without the shoulder strap.

Hazard 4 Tonto – Belt Loop

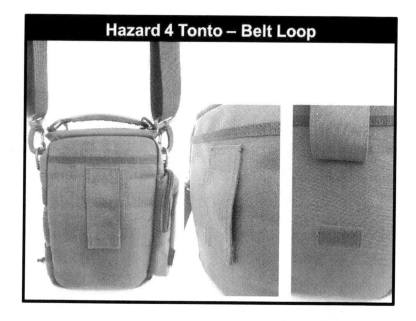

Locking Front Buckle

The front buckle is a very large 2 inch buckle of good quality that has the ability to lock. The locking feature provides an added measure of security for your valuable gear. You can easily manipulate the lock with one hand and then gain access to the bag. On the buckle are the words "Lock" and "Open" so you can easily identify the status of the buckle. To open or lock the buckle you simply slide the mechanism either up or down to the correct position. The buckle is attached to a wide nylon strap that has a D-ring on the bottom. This strap can be tightened down to compress the contents of the pack if needed. You could also strap an item of clothing such as a thin jacket in this area. Both the buckle and large D-ring are made of a durable plastic that should last for the life of the bag.

Hazard 4 Tonto – Buckle

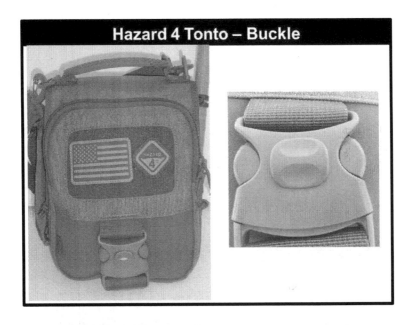

Hazard 4 Tonto – D-Ring

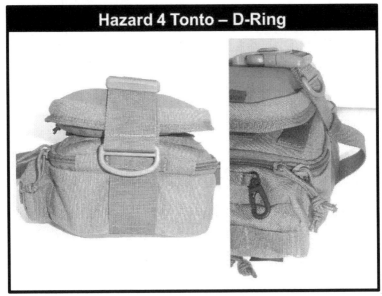

Back Slip Pocket

The back of the Tonto has a slip pocket that is very concealed and potentially easy to miss as it blends into the pack well. If you did not look closely it would appear that the top of the pocket is just an area that consists of stitching for the pack. The pocket is secured closed with Velcro. The pocket is essentially the width and length of the back of the pack but it is very thin. This is generally not a pocket for gear and is more suitable to thin items such as important papers like your emergency communications plan. A thin fixed blade knife would also work and possibly a very small, thin profile pistol. It you were to place a bulky item in this pocket it would print to the outside and potentially leave less room for gear in the main compartment.

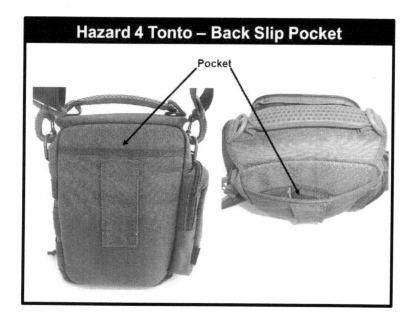

Hazard 4 Tonto – Back Slip Pocket

Pocket

Front Flap Pocket

The Hazard 4 Tonto is considered a *"concealed carry mini-messenger bag."* If you wanted to carry a firearm this would be the pocket to use. As I am dedicating this pack to a ham radio go bag I do not put a firearm in this bag. But, in an emergency situation you may want to carry a firearm. The reason that I do not include one in this set up is because this bag is my "Comms Bag" which is one part of a larger system where I incorporate my firearm. If you are using this as a stand-alone system and you do not carry a firearm on your person then you may choose to use this pocket to carry a firearm.

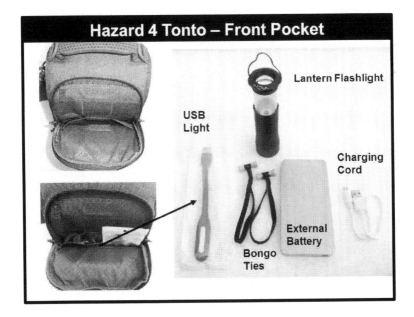

Hazard 4 Tonto – Front Pocket

Lantern Flashlight

USB Light

Charging Cord

External Battery

Bongo Ties

Ham Radio Go Bag

In this front pocket I carry the following items:

- USB Light

- Lantern / Flashlight Combination

- External Battery that is 12,000 mAh's

- Phone Charging Cord

- Set of 10 Bongo Ties to Secure Items

Admin Area

The admin area consists of numerous organizational pocket for accessories as well as a pocket on the front flap that has a transparent cover. You can place a map in this area or other items that you may need to refer to during your situation. I also carry a copy of my FCC Amateur Radio license in this area.

In the admin area I carry the following items:

- Extra phone charging cable

- Radio cloning cable

- 12 volt DC adaptor for a cigarette lighter

- External microphone

- Extra radio battery

- Antenna adapter

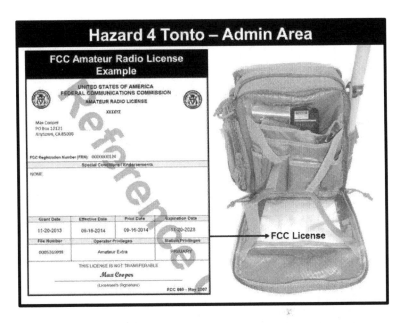

Hazard 4 Tonto – Admin Area

FCC Amateur Radio License Example

FCC License

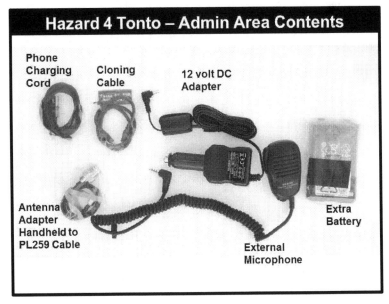

Hazard 4 Tonto – Admin Area Contents

Phone Charging Cord

Cloning Cable

12 volt DC Adapter

Antenna Adapter Handheld to PL259 Cable

External Microphone

Extra Battery

Side Slip Pocket

The side slip pocket typically holds the Diamond SRH77CA antenna that is secured in a protective PCV case and secured in place with a Bongo Tie. When I am using the antenna I will put a SOG Specialty Knives & Tools SwitchPlier Multi-tool 2.0 either in the slip pocket or attach it to the outside of the pocket using the MOLLE webbing. Because this SOG tool has a pocket clip it is easy to attach to the MOLLE on the outside of the pocket which you would not be able to do with a different multi-tool that does not have a clip. You could attach a MOLLE pouch but that adds a little more bulk and weight. Options are good to have so feel free to attach separate pouch if it fits your needs.

The SOG Specialty Knives & Tools SwitchPlier Multi-tool 2.0 has 12 tools. It is made from 420 stainless Steel and has as approximately .38% carbon which means that this steel is very soft and doesn't hold an edge well. On the plus side all 420 stainless steel is extremely rust resistant which may be beneficial depending on your location.

SwitchPlier 2.0 Specifications:

- Closed length: 4.3 inches
- Open Length: 6.1 inches
- Weight 6.3 ounces
- Finish: Stain and Black
- Steel: 420 Stainless Steel

Following is my breakdown of all the tools:

- Pliers: The pliers are the highlight of the SwitchPlier 2.0 as it is very easy to deploy and functions well. When the unit is closed you simple depress a button to activate the pliers to the open position. Once open the handle design and the angle of the pliers make it very functional and easy to use especially one handed.

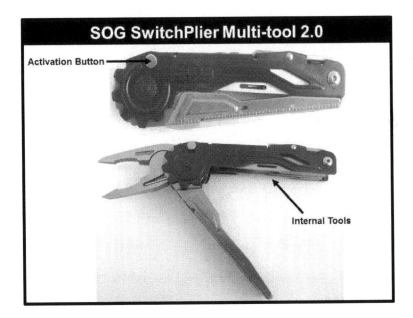

- Wire Cutter: Works well for the wires that I cut. I had no problem cutting through multiple sized wires. The cut was very smooth.

Ham Radio Go Bag

- Ruler: The ruler is located on the handle and has both inches and centimeters. The numbers are small to read and not very beneficial.

- Bottle Opener: Works well.

- Medium Screwdriver: Works well but does not have a lot of reach.

- Can Opener: Works well but is a bit on the small size.

- Small Screwdriver: Works well but does not have a lot of reach.

- Awl: The awl is very sharp and works great.

- Phillips Screwdriver: Works well and has a little more reach than the other screwdrivers.

- 3 Sided File: This file is not big but I really like it as it works very nicely for small tasks. I also like having a file on the edge which provides a very small file area that comes in handy.

- Half Serrated Blade: The blade came relatively sharp but has a very cheap feel to it. Being that it is 420 steel I would not recommend much abuse with the blade. Also, this should not be a primary blade as it just is not big enough or strong enough. I would have preferred just a straight edge instead of the serrated blade. Being that I will have a primary knife on my person the blade on the SwitchPlier is really just a backup.

- Low Profile Pocket Clip: The pocket clip is very nice as is most of SOG's pocket clips. When in the pocket you barely will see the tool which is a nice feature. The clip is a little weaker than some of their other clips meaning that is will bend if the clip is pulled in the wrong direction. In the case of this back it is very easy to attach the pocket clip to the MOLLE webbing.

Accessing the internal tools can be a bit of a challenge as when you grab one tool all of the rest of the tools want to come out as well. When you open your desired tool you can then close the pliers so that it does not remain open. This will provide you a better grip when using the chosen tool.

The SwitchPlier Multi-tool 2.0 provides a very easy and convenient method of accessing the pliers and this appears to be the main functionality of this tool. It is nice that you can open the pliers one handed especially when your other hand is busy. When opening the pliers there is not a big jolt so the tool should not accidently fall out of your hand. Closing the pliers is also easy. Accessing the internal tools can be a bit of a challenge but not a huge deal. As this tool comes with a pocket clip there is no external carry case and one is not needed.

Choose a multi-tool that meets your needs.

Side Slip Pocket

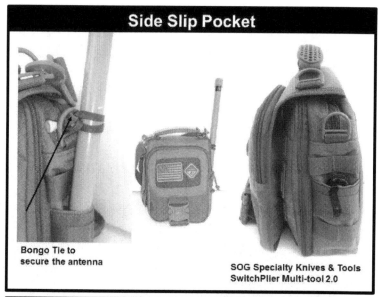

Bongo Tie to
secure the antenna

SOG Specialty Knives & Tools
SwitchPlier Multi-tool 2.0

SOG SwitchPlier Multi-tool 2.0

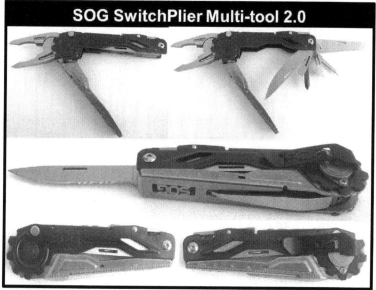

Side Pocket

The pocket on the side of the Tonto has MOLLE on the outside and metal snap-hook. Internally, the pocket is designed for smaller items about the size of a 12 ounce can of soda. This pocket includes and internal sleeve to place small items. In this pocket I carry the GP-5 SSB General Purpose Radio sold at County Comm.[xvii] Following are the radio specifications listed on the County Comm website:

Specs:

- Radio: 225 hrs at 40% Volume
- FM – Stereo via stereo earphones / MW / LW / SW
- FM Frequency range adjustable (76 / 87 / 87.5 ~ 108 MHz)
- Antenna Length 18 Inches
- 450 Station Memories [Actually has 550]
- Multi Tuning Methods: ATS, ETM, Auto scan tuning with 5 seconds pre-listening for both frequency & memory (VF / VM), Manual tuning 9K/10K AM tuning step selectable
- Silicon Labs Si4734 DSP chipset
- LCD Backlight
- Key lock function
- External AM antenna Jack
- Built-in rechargeable function (USB jack, 5V) (can use rechargeable batteries)

Ham Radio Go Bag

- Size: 53 (W) x 159 (H) x 26 (D) mm

Modes: AM, FM, SW, USB, LSB

- **FM**: 87 – 108 or 76 – 108 MHz
- **MW / AM**: 522 - 1620 (9K tuning step) or 520 – 1710 kHz (10K tuning step)
- **SW**: Extended Frequency Range to 1711-29999 (higher and lower coverage)
- **LW** frequency: 150 – 522 kHz (available for 9K tuning step only)

Accessories include:

- Stereo earphones
- External AM antenna
- Soft antenna
- Carrying pouch
- User manual

Power Requirements:

- 4.5 Volts DC via side jack (no adapter included)
- 3 each "AA" batteries
- Dimensions: 6.20" X 2.05" X .80"
- Weight: 85 Grams not including batteries
- Speaker: 40 mm in diameter, 4 Ohms, .5 watt
- Earphone Jack: 3.5 MM, Earphones Included

GP-5 SSB General Purpose Radio

Hazard 4 Tonto – Side Pocket

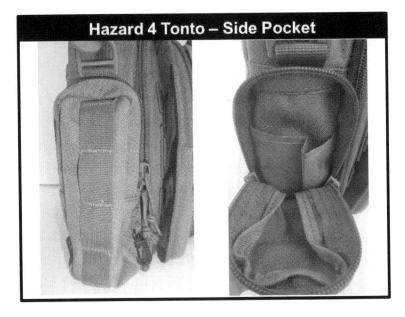

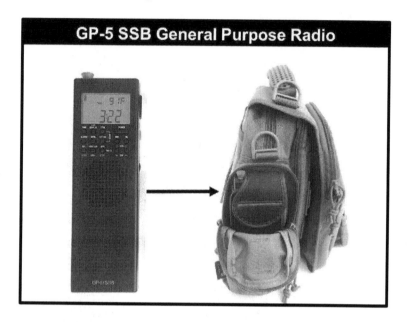

The GP-5 / SSB General Purpose Radio is a relatively small radio that is packed with useful features and functionality. The more I use this radio the more I like it. In times of a crisis or emergency information is an extremely valuable commodity that can help with decision making. This radio is just another tool that can potentially help you gather relevant information and guide your course of action.

In the side pocket I carry the following items:

- Stereo earphones
- External AM antenna
- Soft antenna
- Carrying pouch
- Extra "Green Tip" Antenna

Aspects about this radio that I like include:

- Very big display that is easy to see and has a bright backlight

- Temperature indicator – This is a nice feature although it seems to be off 1-4 degrees which I do not find problematic. The temperature can be displayed in Fahrenheit or Celsius.

- Time is displayed

- The display can show signal strength and signal noise to ratio

- Includes sleep timer and alarm

- Has a key lock function

- Significant amount of memory and it is very easy to store and delete memory. There are a total of 550 memories as follows:

    - 100 FM
    - 100 MW
    - 100 SSB
    - 250 SW

- Easy Tuning Mode (ETM) is an absolute great feature that will scan and temporarily store stations that you can choose to then store in permanent memory. I own a few MW and SW radios and the ETM feature works great. Additionally, the scan is relatively fast. Of all the features on this radio I find that the ETM is one of the most valuable.

- Includes Upper Side Band (USB) and Lower Side Band (LSB) which is a nice feature in this radio. Also has BFO mode for increased tuning.

- Two external antenna's:

    - External FM/SW antenna that clips on to the telescopic antenna

    - External AM/LW antenna that plugs into the AM antenna jack

- Uses 3 AA batteries which are common, inexpensive, and easy to find. You can also use a USB 5V DC IN jack. Can use NiMH batteries and charge while in radio.

The speaker quality is not great but it is not bad for a small speaker. It sounds much better with headphones but headphones may not be possible depending on the situation. In an emergency it may not be a good idea to wear headphones and virtually eliminate one of your critical senses. If you are with a group this might not be as big a factor.

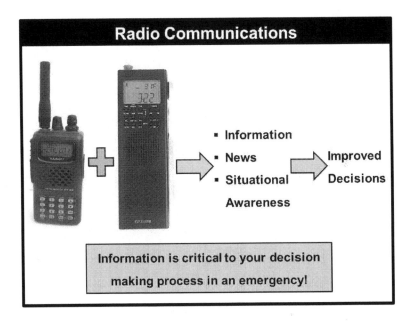

Radio Communications

- Information
- News
- Situational Awareness

→ Improved Decisions

Information is critical to your decision making process in an emergency!

Main Compartment

The main compartment is where I store my radio and other radio accessories. It has an adjustable main-compartment padded-divider which provides an added layer of protection to the front of my radio. There are two small pockets on the sides of the main compartment that allow me to store a radio antenna in each opening.

I keep the important radio items in the main compartment because it provides the most protection from damage. I purposefully do not overfill this section to keep the pack light and to add additional items depending on the situation. As with all my packs they are very dynamic and change as necessary.

Ham Radio Go Bag

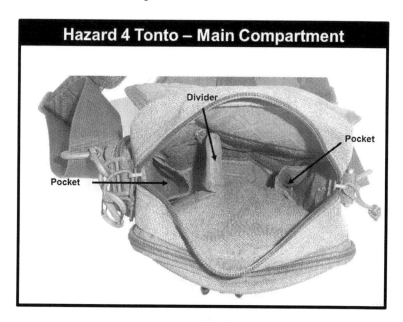

Hazard 4 Tonto – Main Compartment

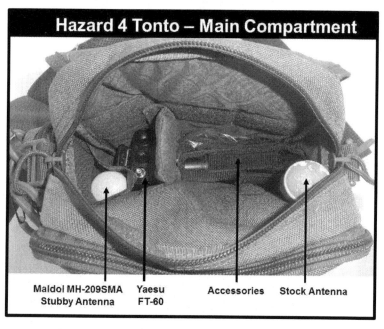

Hazard 4 Tonto – Main Compartment

Maldol MH-209SMA Stubby Antenna   Yaesu FT-60   Accessories   Stock Antenna

Hazard 4 Tonto – Main Compartment Contents

If you are designing a ham radio go bag as a "stand-alone" system then you may choose to add more items to your set-up. If you are designing your radio go bag as one component of a larger more complete system then you will tend to focus solely on the radio and related accessories. The beauty is that you have complete creative authority to determine the eventual outcome of your system. Therefore, do not focus on imitating what another person has designed as their system because it would be rare that you have the exact same skills, experience, or circumstances. While imitation is referred to as the "highest form of flattery" it also means that you may not be prepared for emergencies that you encounter. This is never a good situation to be in especially if lives are at stake.

Tip: I highly recommend using a label maker to identify all of your radio equipment. You can use your FCC Callsign on the label to identify the equipment as your own. It is potentially easy to lose items of gear that are not properly marked and identified.

Maxpedition Remora GearSlinger[xviii]

Maxpedition is a company known for making high quality products. They have a very dedicated and loyal customer base. I own and have used and abused a lot of Maxpedition gear and all of their products hold up very well. The Remora GearSlinger is no exception and is an option to consider for your Ham Radio Go Bag. Material, workmanship, stitching, zippers, etc. are excellent. In addition, Maxpedition has a wide variety of different products that may fit your needs.

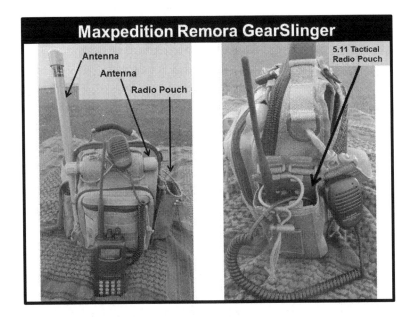

Maxpedition Remora GearSlinger

Ham Radio Go Bag

According to the Maxpedition website the follow information is listed regarding the Remora GearSlinger:

Product Dimensions

- Overall size: 8"(L) x 5"(W) x 10"(H)

- Volume: 320 cu.in. / 5.2L

Product Materials

- 1000-Denier water and abrasion resistant light-weight ballistic nylon fabric

- Teflon™ fabric protector for grime resistance and easy maintenance

- High strength zippers and zipper tracks

- UTX-Duraflex nylon buckles for low sound closures

- Triple polyurethane coated for water resistance

- High tensile strength nylon webbing

- High tensile strength composite nylon thread (stronger than ordinary industry standard nylon thread)

- #AS-100 high grade closed-cell foam padding material for superior shock protection

- Internal seams taped and finished

- Paracord zipper pulls

- Stress points double stitched, Bartacked or "Box-and-X" stitched for added strength

The Maxpedition Remora GearSlinger is a solid option for your ham radio go bag. Maxpedition has an excellent reputation for quality gear that will last a lifetime. All of the equipment discussed previously with the Hazard 4 Tonto setup will also fit in the Maxpedition Remora. This is just a different platform.

Clearly, the setup, design, and organization is different with the Maxpedition Remora compared to the Hazard 4 Tonto. Yet, both are high quality products that are well made and will last a very long time. This will be the case with most quality platforms that you research unless you are looking at product clones. Be very careful of product clones. These are products that "look" the same as a name brand name product but are typically offered at a substantially lower price. With this lower price comes significantly lower quality! When you purchase lower quality products do not expect them to perform or last as long as the name brand items. Quality comes with a price for a reason. ***Therefore, I strongly disagree with the concept of buying cheap gear.*** This is especially true when it comes to purchasing a ham radio. I have done it in the past and it <u>NEVER</u> works out well. The outcome is <u>ALWAYS</u> bad. And in the long run you end up spending the money for quality gear to replace the cheap ineffective gear.

> **If your life is at stake during an emergency situation would you rather have an inexpensive radio that does not perform well or high quality radio that is reliable and dependable?**

In my experience I have always ended up replacing cheap gear with quality gear because the cheap gear does not work, fails to last, or does not perform as designed. The quality of cheap gear is not worth the lower price. When my butt is on the line this is unacceptable. There is not much worse than having a ham radio go bag full of useless gear or a substandard radio that will not perform when needed most and not finding out until you use it. When it comes to gear get the best quality that you can afford. If it comes down to having nothing for the time being then save your money until you can get what you need so that you cannot only depend on the gear but have confidence in its ability.

There is no substitute for quality!

The Trap of Brand Loyalty

Like many of you, I really enjoy gear of all types. I have different gear set up for different situations as a *"one size fits all"* is rarely a feasible reality. I am constantly on the lookout for the next and best piece of equipment that will bring my gear hunt to an end. Experience has taught me that this is an unrealistic expectation. The reality is that new products are constantly being designed, manufactured, marketed, and advertised. One excellent example is the SHOT Show that takes place every year in Las Vegas. Companies pack the halls to showcase their next best piece of gear. The ultimate goal of these companies is to get you to spend your hard earned money on their products and not their competitor's products. And it usually works very well. It is capitalism at its finest. God bless America for providing a variety of high quality products.

Some "gear hunters" fall into the trap of brand loyalty and then stick with one company at the exclusion of all others. I see this across different companies such as: Yaesu, Icom, Kenwood, Hazard 4, Maxpedition, 5.11 Tactical, Blackhawk, SureFire, Streamlight, Glock, Colt, Sig Sauer, etc. The list can go on and on for a variety of different genres of gear. Even I have fallen into this trap a time or two. But not anymore because it is limiting and not to my benefit. When you fall into the trap of brand loyalty you become very myopic and miss out on the opportunity to obtain great quality gear and products from a variety of different companies. This makes no sense and only limits you in your quest for the best, most functional and most utilitarian gear.

Like many situations in life you must remain open to new ideas. Learn to become flexible and adaptable to changing markets, companies, and products. It is always wise to keep your options open. Variety is the spice of life so they say. You state:

"But I love my (fill in the blank brand.)"

Fine, if you have a company that makes great gear <u>that fits your needs</u> then buy from them. But, do not exclude other options from different companies especially if they are a better fit for your particular needs. Also, remember that competition among gear companies is very real. Companies that fail to create and produce quality products that fit customer needs tend to go away. When quality slips from a good company or fails to improve from a substandard company then they will eventually go out of business – as they should. If you stick with one company because they make a great product that fits your needs then don't sweat it. Sticking with them because you feel obligated for whatever reason indicates that it is time to reconsider your options. If companies want you to maintain brand loyalty then they need to continually produce superior products at a reasonable and fair price. Gear is big business and it is up to the companies to live up to <u>our</u> expectations. As consumers you decide who stays and who goes out of business based on where you spend your money. Commercial Darwinism at its finest.

When choosing gear look at product reviews but realize that the person writing the review may have significantly different needs than you. Also, some reviewers write a negative review because they do not understand the functionality of the product and then write a review that is not accurate to the products capability. When it comes to reviews just accept that some may not be accurate for your situation. Another option is to talk with people who already own the product to see what the person feels are the pros and cons of the item. Having the opportunity to talk with someone can provide you with significant product insight. Depending on what product you are looking to purchase consider examining the following elements: product material, workmanship, knobs, buttons, connectors, accessories, display, zippers, stitching, straps, padding, pocket size, organization, product specifications, color, user manual, ability to add on components, durability, warranty, customer service, etc. You should spend time examining the product to see if it really meets your needs. This is especially true with expensive items such as radios and some packs.

Ham Radio Go Bag

Emergency Communications Plan

Your emergency communications plan (ECP) is really the foundation of your ham radio go bag. This plan along with the assessment that you completed earlier will help guide you in determining your needs for you and your family. It is important to realize that amateur radio communications is only one part of your overall plan and may not be the main focus. Your ECP should be comprehensive and include multiple methods of communication both locally and regionally.

If you have young children it is important to know what their schools emergency plan is so that you can factor this into your plans. It is also critical to go over the plan with your children in an age appropriate manner so that you do not scare or frighten your children which can result in negative and long term consequences such as anxiety and depression. Young children need to know that they are safe and have stability so keep this in mind when discussing the plan with children. As parents, it is our responsibility to ensure that our children feel safe. If you have elderly parents that you are responsible for providing care you must also include them in your plan with the understanding that they may not be able to participate fully do to their age and medical conditions. Young children and elderly parents can complicate the best plan which is why it is important to train and practice your plan. You will also need to be flexible and adaptable to the situations that you encounter.

Ham Radio Go Bag

Emergency Phone Numbers:

Contact	Phone Number
Police, Fire, Paramedics, Ambulance	**9-1-1**
Poison Control Center (U.S.)	800-222-1222

Emergency Meeting Location:

	Location	Notes
Primary		
Secondary		
Out of Town		

Family Contacts:

Family Member	Cell Phone	Alt. Phone	E-Mail

Secondary Emergency Contacts:

Secondary Contact	Cell Phone	Alt. Phone	E-Mail

Out of State Contacts:

Out of State Contact	Cell Phone	Alt. Phone	E-Mail

School Phone Numbers:

School	Main Phone	Alt. Phone

Utility Companies:

Company	Emergency 24 Hour	Main Phone

Ham Radio Go Bag

Other Important Contacts:

Contact	Name	Phone	Policy #
Doctor			
Pharmacy			
Hospital			
Medical Insurance			
Secondary Medical Ins.			
Homeowners Ins.			
Flood Insurance			
Vehicle Insurance			
Pet Insurance			
Bank 1			
Bank 2			
Credit Card 1			
Credit Card 2			
Debit Card			

Pet Emergency Contact Information:

Company	Phone	Notes
Veterinarian		
Emergency Animal Hospital		
Animal Control		
Shelter Option 1		
Shelter Option 2		
Pet Poison Helpline	800-213-6680	$39.00 fee

Pet Information:

Pet Name	Tag #	Notes
		i.e. Microchipped, Allergies

Ham Radio Comms:

Channel #	Channel Name	Band	Frequency	Comms Plan
		2M		
		70cm		

Out of State Ham Radio Contacts:

Call Sign	Channel #	Frequency	Comms Plan

EMCOMM Notes:

_____

_____

_____

_____

_____

_____

_____

_____

_____

_____

Information regarding the previous plan

- Emergency phone numbers:

    List all the possible emergency phone numbers that you may use in a crisis or emergency situation. It is important to include 9-1-1 for police, fire, paramedics, and ambulance because family members may be so stressed out at the situation they forget this phone number. Never discount the impact that stress can have on your emergency plan. And while 9-1-1 will be included on your plan keep in mind that in a large scale emergency the phones may not work or 9-1-1 will be so overwhelmed that you will not be able to get through to these emergency services. You may be on your own for a while. Other potential phone numbers to include on this section may include: American Red Cross, Federal Emergency Management Agency (FEMA), non-emergency number to your local police department, federal law enforcement agencies, disaster relief agencies, etc.

- Emergency Meeting Locations:

    Always include at least three locations to meet with family members in an emergency. Two of these locations should be local and one should be out of town. If you have young children or elderly parents you have to plan on how you are going to transport them to the meeting location. This may be especially difficult if children are at school and a flood of parents are all converging on the school at the same time. It is crucial to actually practice going to the exact specific location you are to meet so that there is no ambiguity as to your meeting location. Also, discuss plans on leaving a message if you were at the location but were unable to stay for some reason and moved on to the secondary meeting point. You may carry a thick black Sharpie marker and discuss where you will leave a message that other family members should look for once they arrive and do not see you once they arrive at the meeting point.

- Family Contacts:

    This is for your immediate family and must include name, cell phone number, alternate phone number if applicable such as a work phone, email address, etc. Consider including contact information for Skype or other such forms of communication. In an emergency situation you may not be able to use these but you never know and options are good.

- Secondary Emergency Contacts:

    This can include extended family and friends who are generally in the same region as you are located. These contacts may not be impacted by the crisis and may be able to assist you and your family.

- Out of State Contacts:

    The crisis or emergency situation may be so bad that you will need the assistance of out of state contacts who can be a hub to pass along messages to other family members. They may also serve as your out of town meeting location. When practicing your Emergency Communications Plan it is important to discuss the role of out of state contacts and how they may be used in a crisis. It is also absolutely critical to inform your out of state contacts that they are part of your ECP and what their role will be during an emergency. Ask the contacts if they agree to be your out of state contact. If not then you will need to find others. It is important to have more than one out of state contact as a contingency plan.

- School Phone Numbers:

Obtain the phone number for each school that you have a child enrolled even if your child is away at college. Inquire to see if the school has a plan for emergency situations. Many schools will say yes but the plan is often very deficient and lacking. Many universities have their own police departments so be sure to obtain the emergency and non-emergency number to contact the police.

- Utility Companies:

Natural disasters and acts of terrorism can impact many utilities. It is important to have their contact information to include their 24 hour emergency hotline. It is also important to know how to turn off your utilities to include electricity, water, and gas.

- Other Important Contacts:

This section can include a wide variety of contact information such as your primary care physician, medical specialists, pharmacy, hospitals, urgent care centers, health insurance, homeowners insurance, bank information, etc. I also highly recommend having an encrypted USB drive with important documents and information. Keep an extra one locked up in a bank vault or safe.

- Pet Emergency Contact Information:

If you own a pet or pets you have a responsibility to ensure that they are taken care of during an emergency. Your pets rely on you 100% for their well-being and you must take this responsibility seriously. It is not an option to leave your pet behind. If you feel it is safe enough to leave your pet at home then you need to stay home as well. Clearly, I view pets as part of the family and not an object. When you get a pet you take on the responsibility to care for the pet all of the time. If you cannot accept this responsibility you should not own a pet. Abandonment of your pet is betrayal and unethical. Pets, especially dogs and cats, should be micro-chipped in case they become lost. Pets that are not micro-chipped who become lost and are then found by animal control are typically euthanized. This is preventable with a microchip and there is no excuse not to have all of your pets chipped. It is part of being a responsible pet owner.

Contact information for pets must include veterinarian, emergency animal hospital, animal control, shelter options (minimum of two), pet poison hotline (there is a $39 dollar fee and you will need a credit/debit card), etc. If you own pets be a responsible owner and ensure for the care and safety of your pets during a crisis.

- Pet Information:

  Include the name, tag number and other relevant information such as if your pet is microchipped, medications, medical conditions, allergies, behavioral issues, etc.

- Ham Radio Comms:

  You should already have a list of frequencies that are programmed into your ham radio. This section can function as a backup or it can include additional frequencies that you may need. This is a good section to include specific frequencies that you will use as part of your ECP. For example, under the "Comms Plan" you might have notes that on a certain frequency you will attempt to make contact with (X) for 5 minutes at the beginning of each hour. This way you specifically know what channel number to be using, what frequency you will be using, and what your plan of action will be.

  In this section include the channel number, channel name, band, frequency, and your comms plan. Remember, the more specific you are with your plan the less room for ambiguity and the less chance for errors and problems.

- Out of State Ham Radio Contacts:

  Just as you have out of state emergency contacts you should consider having out of state ham radio contacts. This will be especially important if the cellular phone network is not working. Using a linked repeater system you can make contact over a very long distance.

This part of your plan must be practiced with the out of state contact to know which repeaters to use and what your plan is going to be to make contact.

- EMCOMM Notes:

    This section is for any other notes that you feel may be relevant to your Family Emergency Communications Plan.

    On your ECP you may also consider including a list of medical conditions, medications, medication allergies and food allergies for you and each family member. You may feel that this section is too personal and may choose to carry it somewhere else and not as part of this plan. Use whatever method works best for your situation.

    The previous emergency communications plan (EMCOMM) is just a sample. Modify the plan to fit your individualized or family needs. I cannot stress how critically important it is to have a written plan and to practice your plan a minimum of two times per year although four times would be much better. It is only through such drills that you will find areas of weakness that need to be modified or fixed. If you fail to train your plan you will find out the weaknesses during a real emergency without the benefit of being able to fix it. This is a situation that is avoidable through training and practice.

    As discussed earlier you should not discount the impact of stress. During a true crisis or emergency you will be under a higher than normal amount of stress. So will your children, elderly parents and pets. Someone needs to be in control and more than likely that person is going to be you. Your family is going to look to you for stability and comfort even when everything may be falling apart. You need to be in control during this time. Panic is contagious and if you panic so will your family. But, if they see that you are in control that will bring a sense of ease to your family. The more you train and have contingency plans the more calm and in control you will be able to remain. It may not be easy especially when a family member become injured or your plan is encountering the cruel hand of Mr. Murphy but you must remain focused.

Ham Radio Go Bag

Summary

When it comes to designing and creating a ham radio go bag, bug out bag, or your everyday carry set up there is no magical one size fits all template. There will always be necessary items to carrying in your system but there is always a lot individuality based on a host of different variables. This is why I consider all of my gear kits very flexible and adaptable. They are in a constant state of change and evaluation even if the changes are very small. Minor improvements in your set up can result in large gains in performance. This is why it is important to always improve your set up when possible. Never become complacent when it comes to your gear and do not settle for mediocrity. This is especially true if your gear is an instrumental part of your emergency plan and can assist with saving lives.

During a crisis, disaster, or emergency you cannot count on cell phone service which may quickly become overwhelmed or completely fail. It is imperative to have alternate forms of communications that will keep you in touch with your loved ones or others. Alternate communications provides you options to gather critical information that helps to guide your decisions. Additionally, I cannot stress the importance of having a written emergency communications plan in your kit. Too often this part is skipped and I find this to be a big mistake. Your plan must be inclusive and practiced for it to be effective. The plan must have emergency phone numbers, meeting locations, evacuation points with back up locations, radio frequencies, out of town contacts, etc. You do not want to learn of your plans weakness during a crisis.

As you can see the kit described in this book mainly contains radio communications equipment. I also have a go bag that has other equipment that I will need in time of a crisis. Redundancy is built into my communications kit when possible by having backup radios and backup power sources consisting of electrical, battery, and solar. Some of these items may be stored in my main bug out bag so that *"all my eggs are not in one basket."* Redundancy for important items helps to mitigate bad things from happening at the worst possible time. During an emergency it is often said that information is power. Having communications provides peace of mind knowing that I will be able to effectively communicate during a crisis. It will provide me with valuable intelligence and information which in turn helps to facilitate more informed decisions.

It is important to keep in mind that there is a significant variance in how you can design your ham radio go bag which is dependent on your overall goals. Use this book as guidance but then develop a system that works for you and will accommodate your individualized factors and variables. I would expect that a ham radio go bag is going to be different for preppers, survivalists, CERT teams, ARES, RACES, preparedness individuals, small groups, etc. Therefore, it is impossible for one setup to meet everyone's unique needs. I have focused on dualband hand held radios that operate in the 2M / 70 cm bands. You may choose to carry a mobile radio such as the Yaesu FT-817 which covers HF, VHF, and UHF bands which is a self-contained battery-powered multi-mode portable transceiver. There are many radio options to choose as well as your platform and radio accessories. Use the information provided in this book as a template and then fill in the blanks based on your needs, license level, skill and other factors.

Keep in mind that the premise of my kit is one that is:

- Based on a 5 watt handy talkie (HT)

- Mobile (meaning easy to transport)

- Simple

- Relatively small

- Lightweight

- Effective

Therefore every item of gear you choose has a size, weight, and utility component that must be examined to ensure that it fits in your set up.

- Too heavy and it becomes difficult to carry. This is especially true if you are in poor physical condition.

- Too bulky and you end up leaving it at home. Or, you carry it with you and lose mobility.

- Lack of functionality and you cannot communicate when you need to communicate.

Ham Radio Go Bag

There is a cost / benefit ratio for every item of gear and it is imperative that you factor this into your decisions when considering what to include in your ham radio go bag. It is critical to understand the pros and cons of the equipment that you carry. Always try to increase the pros while minimizing the cons. I also believe that there are some cons that should never be overlook. For example, you may own radio that has many features that you like but the one con is poor quality control leading to performance issues. This one con should negate all the pros. Therefore, you should not choose this radio. Yet, I see this happening all of the time when people purchase cheap ham radios and overlook poor performance. It does not make sense that a radio for emergency situations would overlook performance that is not reliable. Preppers, survivalists, and amateur radio operators should never accept "cons" that may result in the loss of life. In other words:

"The worst case scenario depends on the best possible performance from both the operator and the gear."

Communications is the one topic that repeatedly comes up when people talk about an area of preparedness that needs to be improved. It is also an area that does require some level of technical ability. Now is the time to start learning, preparing and developing this necessary set of skills. Think back to the brief scenario that began this book. You do not want to be in the dark. As was stated at the end of the scenario:

The dark can be a scary and lonely place...especially for the unprepared!

Remember the adage:

Failing to plan is planning to fail.

Shine light in your areas of darkness by acquiring the necessary knowledge, skills and abilities that will keep you and your family alive in an emergency. Then you need to practice, practice, and practice some more. There are no shortcuts.

Good luck, stay safe and build a ham radio go bag that works for you.

Ham Radio Go Bag

Go Bag Checklist

- ☐ Handy Talky (HT) Radio Dual-Band 2M / 70cm
- ☐ Antenna
- ☐ Spare antenna
- ☐ All local repeaters pre-programmed and tested
- ☐ Laminated sheet of all frequencies
- ☐ Laminated copy of FCC Amateur Radio license
- ☐ Emergency communications plan
- ☐ Radio instruction manual or cheat sheet
- ☐ Handheld microphone
- ☐ Headphones
- ☐ 12 volt DC adapter, i.e. cigarette lighter
- ☐ AC adapter
- ☐ Spare radio battery
- ☐ Alkaline battery case
- ☐ 12 alkaline AA batteries
- ☐ Radio cloning cable
- ☐ Handheld to PL259 Cable
- ☐ Bongo Ties – 10 pack
- ☐ Electrical tape
- ☐ Notepad and writing instrument (I like Rite in the Rain and Fisher Space Pens)
- ☐ Shortwave radio

Ham Radio Go Bag

ITU Phonetic Alphabet

Letter	Word	Pronunciation
A	Alfa	**AL** FAH
B	Bravo	**BRAH** VOH
C	Charlie	**CHAR** LEE
D	Delta	**DELL** TAH
E	Echo	**ECK** OH
F	Foxtrot	**FOKS** TROT
G	Golf	GOLF
H	Hotel	HOH **TELL**
I	India	**IN** DEE AH
J	Juliet	**JEW** LEE ETT
K	Kilo	**KEY** LOH
L	Lima	**LEE** MAH
M	Mike	MIKE
N	November	NO **VEM** BER
O	Oscar	**OSS** CAH
P	Papa	PAH **PAH**
Q	Quebec	KEH **BECK**
R	Romeo	**ROW** ME OH
S	Sierra	SEE **AIR** RAH
T	Tango	TANG GO
U	Uniform	**YOU** NEE FORM
V	Victor	**VIK** TAH
W	Whiskey	**WISS** KEY
X	X-Ray	**ECKS** RAY
Y	Yankee	**YANG** KEY
Z	Zulu	**ZOO** LOO

Ham Radio Go Bag

Morse Code

While Morse Code is no longer a requirement to obtain your amateur radio license it can still be a valuable skill to learn. Remember, FCC Rule, **§97.113 Prohibited Transmissions**[xix] states that you are prohibited from using:

"(4) …; messages encoded for the purpose of obscuring their meaning"

You may be in a situation where using some form of a "coded" message is valuable but this is not allowed per FCC rules. But, Morse code is an acceptable form of communication and is permitted with amateur radio. It can be an effective way to communicate with others in a manner that may be cryptic to those who do not understand Morse code. Just keep in mind that your message is not private and there are people who will be able to understand your message.

There are many online tools available and phone apps, for free, that will help you learn Morse code. Consider this another tool in the toolbox that may come in handy. A quick internet and app search will reveal many resources that are available to learn Morse code.

> Morse Code Message:
>
> -- --- .-. ... . / -.-. --- -.. . / -.-. .- -. / -... . / .- /
>
> ...- .- .-.. ..- .- -... .-.. . / - --- --- .-.. .-.-.-

International Morse Code

1. A dash is equal to three dots.
2. The space between parts of the same letter is equal to one dot.
3. The space between two letters is equal to three dots.
4. The space between two words is equal to seven dots.

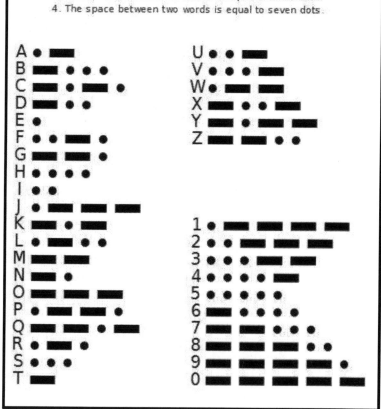

About the Author

Max Cooper is a pseudonym for an individual who has held many positions within the criminal justice system and has extensive experience in officer safety and survival. He has experience in probation, parole and corrections. Throughout his career he was an officer survival instructor and was integral in the development and implementation of officer safety curriculum for two large agencies.

He served as a Certified Firearms Instructor, Lead Defensive Tactics instructor, and has a black belt in three martial arts. He taught classes on: Use of Force, Tactical Mindset, Applied Defensive Tactics, Low-light Shooting, Force-on-Force, Judgmental Shooting, Verbal De-escalation, Safety Policies, and other courses. He has consulted and provided training for probation and court departments on staff safety. Mr. Cooper has worked with numerous municipal, county, state, and federal law enforcement agencies relating to probation and parole. He has trained with the Federal Bureau of Investigations (FBI), numerous Police and Sheriff's Departments, SureFire Institute, and many other government and private agencies on topics to include: officer survival, active shooter intervention, force-on-force training, shoot house instructor, terrorism, weapons of mass destruction, building searches, school violence, workplace violence, flashbang operator, tactical scouting, and others. He has also received specialized training on the topics of: Sex Offenders, Domestic Violence Offenders, Mental Health Offenders, Critical Incident Stress Debriefing, Motivational Interviewing, Risk and Needs Assessments, Public Information Officer training, numerous leadership schools, Faculty Skills Development, Advanced Faculty Skills Development, and Curriculum & Lesson Plan Development.

Mr. Cooper has received Supervisor of the Year, Exceptional Service Award, Director's Team Award, Trainer Excellence Awards, Letters of Commendation, and was nominated for Officer of the Year on two occasions. He has a Master's of Education Degree and a Bachelor of Science in Business.

Books by Max Cooper

- Realistic Bug Out Bag

- Realistic Everyday Carry

- Everyday Carry: 5.11 Tactical PUSH Pack

- Desert Survival Kit

- Minimalist Survival Kit

- Prepper Survival: Debunked, Why Most Preppers Won't Survive

- Prepper Training Workbook

Ham Radio Go Bag

Resources

- **ARRL**

  http://www.arrl.org/home

- **FCC Universal Licensing System**

  http://wireless2.fcc.gov/UlsApp/UlsSearch/searchLicense.jsp

- **Part 97: Amateur Radio Service**

  http://www.gpo.gov/fdsys/pkg/CFR-2009-title47-vol5/pdf/CFR-2009-title47-vol5-part97.pdf

- **International Amateur Radio Union (IARU)**

  http://www.iaru.org/

- **Technician Level Question Pool for 2014-2018**

  http://ncvec.org/page.php?id=362

Ham Radio Go Bag

- **Chart of US Amateur Radio Technician Privileges:**

  http://www.arrl.org/files/file/Tech%20Band%20Char
  t/Tech%20Band%20Chart.pdf

- **Yaesu**

  https://www.yaesu.com/

- **Kenwood**

  http://www.kenwoodusa.com/Communications/Ama
  teur_Radio/

- **Icom**

  http://www.icomamerica.com/en/amateur/

- **Ham Radio Outlet**

  http://www.hamradio.com/

- **Universal Radio**

  http://www.universal-radio.com/

- **Ham City**

  https://www.hamcity.com/store/pc/home.asp

- **QRZ.com**

  http://www.qrz.com/

- **eHam.net**

  http://www.eham.net/

- **EchoLink**

  http://www.echolink.org/

- **ERT Electronics and Radio Today**

  http://www.electronics-radio.com/

- **Learn Morse Code**

  http://www.learnmorsecode.com/

Ham Radio Go Bag

References

[i] http://www.fcc.gov/

[ii] http://www.ecfr.gov/cgi-bin/text-idx?c=ecfr&tpl=/ecfrbrowse/Title47/47cfrv5_02.tpl

[iii] http://www.gpo.gov/fdsys/pkg/CFR-2009-title47-vol5/pdf/CFR-2009-title47-vol5-sec97-113.pdf

[iv] http://www.fcc.gov/encyclopedia/general-mobile-radio-service-gmrs

[v] http://hamexam.org/

[vi] http://www.arrl.org/news/2012-marks-all-time-high-for-amateur-radio-licenses

[vii] Amateur Radio Emergency Service (ARES) is a corps of trained amateur radio operator volunteers organized to assist in public service and emergency communications. It is organized and sponsored by the American Radio Relay League and the Radio Amateurs of Canada.

[viii] RACES is a radio communications service, conducted by volunteer licensed amateur radio operators, for providing emergency communications support to State and local governments.

[ix] http://transition.fcc.gov/pshs/services/amateur.html

[x] http://www.gpo.gov/fdsys/pkg/CFR-2009-title47-vol5/pdf/CFR-2009-title47-vol5-part97-subpartE.pdf

[xi] http://www.gpo.gov/fdsys/pkg/CFR-2011-title47-vol5/pdf/CFR-2011-title47-vol5-sec97-501.pdf

[xii] http://www.arrl.org/getting-your-technician-license

[xiii] http://wireless.fcc.gov/uls/index.htm?job=home

[xiv] https://itunes.apple.com/app/echolink/id350688562?mt=8

[xv] http://wireless2.fcc.gov/UlsApp/UlsSearch/searchLicense.jsp

[xvi] http://hazard4.com/products/bags/messengers/tonto

[xvii] http://www.countycomm.com/gp5ssb.html

---

xviii http://www.maxpedition.com/store/pc/REMORA-GEARSLINGER-3p384.htm
xix http://www.gpo.gov/fdsys/pkg/CFR-2009-title47-vol5/pdf/CFR-2009-title47-vol5-sec97-113.pdf

Made in the USA
Lexington, KY
06 July 2018